Getting to Know You

Prayer and God

by
ETTA GULLICK

Gift of author, a friend of fr. Louis Merton.

T F

First published in Great Britain in 1976 by
MAYHEW-McCRIMMON LTD
Great Wakering, Essex

©Copyright 1976 by Etta Gullick

Reprinted 1982

ISBN 0 85597 100 2

The author and publisher gratefully acknowledge permission
given by the Oxford Diocesan Magazine to base some of the
chapters in this book on articles which originally appeared in
that magazine. They are also grateful to Kenneth Woolcombe,
Bishop of Oxford for suggesting that the articles should be
written in the first place.

Cover design: Paul Chilvers
Printed in Hong Kong by
Permanent Typesetting & Printing Co., Ltd.

Contents

Relating in Honesty

A number of people think that prayer is only for the virtuous and holy, and not for us who struggle rather half-heartedly to follow Christ. I think we often forget that Jesus ate and drank with tax-collectors and sinners, and he did this persistently and that they were people who had really sinned often in unpleasant and sordid ways. His friends included the publican who had probably taken bribes, sinners who had got drunk, slept with whores, and other people who had shocked the righteous of the day. Christ met people at their point of need, where they really wanted help. He did not go to the righteous who considered themselves virtuous and without need, but to those who acknowledged what sort of people they were and made no pretence about it.

Perhaps some of the prayers in books which have been used until recently have suggested that God only wished us to pray for certain things and in set ways, and were only for when we were feeling holy. The things prayed for often seemed far removed from our needs and desires, and the ways suggested were often framed in pious, out-moded language which most certainly is not ours today.

Many people seem to have been put off by such books or these sort of prayers because they felt they were not 'them' and thought that it would be hypocritical to use them. If they had looked at the Psalms, or at the people in the Old Testament who talked to God person to person and argued with him, they would have had a better idea what prayer, that is talking and relating to God, could be like. It consists of being honest with God, having a personal relationship with him which is open and natural and does not start with pious deceptions. Christ said that the publican's prayer 'God be merciful to me a sinner' was more profitable for him than that of the Pharisee, who thanked God that he was not like the sinners of his race. The publican knew what he was like and knew that God knew this too, and made no bones about it, but honestly asked for God's help and mercy. Throughout the gospels Jesus gives hints about prayer, never rules, and if we read and look with eyes and minds open, we will find clues about prayer from Jesus' words and from the way he lived.

Like the publican, we do not come to God perfect, having put away evil; we come to be delivered from the evil which wars with the good in our being. God can come into our situation if we pray honestly, even if we swear at him or ask for things which we may know are not right, or things we are not sure about. We may come to God with passion raging in our hearts, saying 'this is what I feel', or 'this is what I want', and wait before him knowing that he will not turn us away but that he will sympathise and help. Of course he cannot sympathise with evil, but he sympathises with us in our struggles with temptations, in our longings and failures. If we are honest with God, he can touch us, change us, relate to us, for honesty allows us to enter into a relationship with him. The Pharisee's self-satisfaction and self-deception made it impossible for him to have an open relationship with God. It is better to pray honestly like Saint Augustine, 'Make me chaste, make me pure — but not yet'. We all know how God ultimately changed him, but we are usually not as honest in our prayer as St. Augustine, nor do we have the courage to add 'not yet' to our requests for goodness for ourselves. We can learn, perhaps gradually, through praying and laying our situation before God what needs to be changed in us, and the more we change, the more God shows us what he wishes to be changed. This process of change in us can be never-ending and on-going if we are honest!

What I am suggesting is, that if you have not done much praying, you start as you are with no pretence, a twentieth century person, often torn with doubt, far from being perfect, living in an uncertain and unsettled world. You will probably be preoccupied with modern problems such as unbelief, permissiveness, the inadequacy of institutional religion, the social injustices of the world, poverty, starvation, strikes, violence and such like. Pray to God from this kind of world, or the world as you know it if you live in a quiet place, use your own words or the prayers of someone else which express your feelings and your attitude. We are all touched in some way or other by the climate of the world we live in, provided we are not enclosed in an ivory tower. We have to pray as we are and as we can at the time of praying, and bring our world with us so as to bring God into it.

Probably you know people who do not believe intellectually in God, yet wish to pray. For many people today do not really seem to know whether they believe in God or not. If they are honest intellectually, they feel they should not pray to a God who seems dead to them. Yet intuitively they feel a need to reflect on life in the presence of some Ultimate Reality. For example Walt Whitman addressed some of his poems to 'You whoever you are' and Dag Hammarskjöld said 'at some moment I did say "yes" to someone or something'. We live in an age of great uncertainty and confusion, and this is bound to affect our prayer. One writer on prayer has said recently 'the night of the spirit has been democratized'. By this he meant that it is not only an elect body of contemplatives who experience darkness in prayer, but the entire people of God seem to, in one form or another, and that in this period of cultural transition it is not only prayer forms which have to be changed and relinquished at God's call but even certain expressions of the Christian faith which are not viable for today. We have, he suggests, to accept fewer forms on our journey to God which will probably be often dark and we will not be quite sure where we are going. We have to pray for this uncertainty in trust, and for many prayer will be more simple and with fewer words than it has been for previous generations.

So I suggest that we have to pray as we can, as we are, and from our situation as it is, in faith and without anxiety. For anxiety is a great enemy of prayer and often arises from an unwillingness to accept our situation as it is. We have to withstand the pressures of ever-threatening despair and let things be as they are. We do not know what God is like — our forefathers had seemingly much more certainty about the nature of God than we have, and we are paying for their desire to make God understandable with the mind and to make him into an idol which we could get hold of, and manipulate for our own ends. People in every age have wanted idols, for there is safety and reassurance in them. And we have the hope that we will be able to manipulate them for our own purposes!

We can learn much from the Old Testament about the elusive, mysterious nature of God. Moses saw God revealed in the bush that burnt and was never consumed; when he asked God his name, he was given a word form, 'I am that I am', or, as that great Jewish mystic, Martin Buber, has translated it, 'I will be there as I will be there', that is 'I will be in every situation, but in a way you may not expect me to be, or in a form which you may not recognise. In fact, you may not realise I am there till later. You cannot make me be there in the way you want me. I will be there, but I will elude your capture'. On the mountain Moses saw God in the darkness or only his back parts, and whatever that may mean, it does suggest that it was an elusive vision. Jacob wrestling with the angel is wounded and the angel gets away without telling him his name, but Jacob is himself given a new name. God is not to be held on to and known as we would like him to be; rather through being in our situation he lets us know something more about ourselves, and helps us with our problems, but not in the way we want or expect. Jacob was able after his struggle with the angel to go on and face Esau without fear though he had been dreading the encounter with his brother. God was in Jacob's situation as he chose to be!

And it is very easy for us to form a preconceived

picture of Jesus, seeing him perhaps as the gentle shepherd, and forgetting how frequently he was incomprehensible and frightening to his disciples. So often we give him the image we would like him to have or the one we expect of him or the one we have seen him given in pictures.

Our encounters with God in prayer can be rather like the Old Testament experiences, if we accept that we will know God as he gives himself to be known and not in the preconceived ways we may expect him to come. And this wrestling with God, this trying to discover who he is and what he is, can be exciting and stimulating though we may never get more than flashes of light or intuitions about him.

It is not easy for us to realise that we pray because God who is always calling us, touches us, and in some manner gets under our guard, and starts us praying. The Holy Spirit is always with us, waiting to help us to pray when we decide we want to! We tend to see all the hard work that we are doing, and get so taken up with it and ourselves that we do not fix our attention on God. We think too much about prayer and not enough about God! It is important to realise and remember always, in prayer time and out, that God loves us, and if we accept this love, we can become more fully ourselves. It is not easy for us to accept as reality that GOD DOES LOVE US whatever we are like and whatever we are doing.

We have to realise and remember too, that we can pray anywhere and at any time, and that prayer and life are not two separate things. We live all our life in the presence of God who loves us, and we have to have faith primarily in the fact that God loves us, and this is, perhaps, more important than believing in God's existence with our minds. We must always keep before us the idea that God loves us, but, as he is far greater than us, his ways will often seem mysterious to us.

So we have to come to prayer as we are, and accept God as he gives himself to us. This implies that prayer is, and will continue to be, a personal encounter with God — a relationship between two persons, one finite and the other infinite, so there is bound to be many elements of darkness, of mystery, and unknowing as well as light in our encounters. We need great faith to accept God in the way he gives himself to us.

It is also very important for us to realise that God plays the major part in our prayer and encounters with him, and that it is the Spirit who prays in us and starts us off praying, and so it is possible to say that most of the work in prayer is God's work.

The God-side of the relationship is always there. God is always with me and that is why the major part of prayer is from God's side and not mine. In any human relationship we have to give time to it, and this is true of our relationship with God. My part is being regular in turning to God, in opening myself to him and in making myself available to him in the knowledge that he is always with me waiting for my response. We do not always realise this, and are, perhaps rather like the elder brother of the prodigal son who had lived all his life with his father but had never asked anything from him, so his father was not able to show him the fullness of his love.

It is fundamental to accept that God is constantly present with us, waiting for us to grow in openness and awareness of his presence. We have to respond to God's love with the whole of our being, mind, body, emotions, instincts, etc., and let him into all our living. We have, as an American friend of mine said, to pray 'total'.

So I suggest that we should be open to God, honest with him, be ourselves with him, hiding nothing, asking and questioning him, and accepting him as he gives himself to us in prayer and life, remembering that the two are always interconnected. If we do this our relationship with God will grow and develop, often in ways that may seem dark and mysterious to us for he is a God who both reveals and hides himself from us for we are too weak to bear the full weight of his glory.

Relating as Whole Persons

Saint Luke in his gospel tells us that the disciples asked Jesus to teach them to pray after they had seen him praying. It was in answer to their request that he taught them what we call 'The Lord's Prayer' or the 'Our Father'. The disciples were seemingly devout Jews who attended synagogue worship weekly, and, one would imagine, had learnt prayers and said psalms there. But obviously they thought there was something different about the prayer of Jesus. It was something that gripped and held him, something he wanted and needed to do, and it was something that helped to make him attractive and gave him power, authority and knowledge of people. It was different from just saying prayers; it was vital and life-giving. I believe that it was different because it was part of a deep, personal, relationship with God, the Father.

Jesus starts the prayer he teaches his disciples with 'Our Father'. Here I believe is the clue why Jesus' prayer was different; it was part of his close personal relationship with God. For this reason, throughout this book, I will keep looking at prayer as a relationship with God.

'Father', I know, can be a rather loaded word today, with overtones and undertones that disturb numbers of people who have not had a good relationship with their fathers, or whose fathers have been impossible or difficult. Today, perhaps, we are more alive to this attitude to fathers, but I think that over the years, men and women have been deterred from our Lord's prayer by the word 'father'. I believe our Lord was suggesting that our relationship with God must be close and intimate. Also a good father or mother loves a baby and cares for it before the baby or child is aware of loving anybody or anything. God loves us before we are even aware of being able to love. God starts the relationship and not us; he initiates and we respond. For some people, it may at the start, be more helpful to regard God as a mother or close friend. The wonderful medieval, English writer, Lady Julian of Norwich, refers to the motherhood of Christ, probably following Saint Anselm, an eleventh century bishop and theologian who had written about the motherhood of Christ before she did. Then, there is the Hebridean saying that there is a mother's heart in the heart of God.

In the prayer he taught his disciples, Jesus wants his followers to realise the closeness and caringness of God's love for them. Saint John uses a word to describe what our attitude to God should be; it is translated in our Bibles 'boldness' or 'confidence' (cf 1Jn. 5.14, 'we are quite confident if we ask him for anything, and it is in accordance with his will, he will hear us'), but it means literally 'saying anything' or 'speaking freely'. It is the attitude of a child to a loving parent; he tells him or her everything honestly, aware that they will understand, care and want to hear, and that they will give him what is best for him. And he has no fear of being misunderstood, for there is trust and love on both sides.

The acceptance of a loving and living relationship with God is what made Jesus' way of praying so different and fascinating to the disciples, and this is the kind of prayer that we should learn to grow into. I believe we should keep looking at Jesus so as to discover how to pray like this.

Also we should remember that the prayer our Lord taught the disciples is an 'our' prayer not a 'my' prayer. Here we pray as we always do, as one of the human family, as a member of the Body of Christ, as belonging to a country, and to smaller groups as well. We pray as people who have a number of relationships. In each of these we relate differently and there are often, seemingly, a number of different 'mes'. In prayer all these different 'mes' are joined in a relationship with God, but they are all there too. We bring our world into the prayer and this includes our relationships, and the problems and joys of human beings who share their humanity to some degree with all other created beings.

My mother used to sing a song in my youth which infuriated me — it seemed so silly to me! As far as I remember it went; 'If you were the only girl in the world and I was the only boy, there would be such wonderful things to do, there would be such wonderful things to say'. I don't believe that two people living without contact with any one else would find it so marvellous; they would probably get quite quickly bored with each other even if they had the plant and animal world! Who can tell? Anyway we do not live like this. Even when we are alone with God, we are part of a community, and we pray as people who have relationships of some kind or other with a number of others.

And if our relationship with God grows deeper, somehow, I believe, our human relationships do too. If we are touched by the wonder and glory of God, this will somehow affect others.

To return to prayer as Jesus did it; he went away regularly to be with his Father, in a deep personal way. We too, if we give time to it regularly, can grow in love for God and to develop a closer relationship with him. God is always with us waiting for us to turn to him but many things can prevent us from responding. We get preoccupied with the activities of daily living and do not find time in the day for God, and when we have finished them we are too tired for prayer. We can discover so many excuses for not praying. We are rather like the people in the gospel story who found such plausible reasons to prevent them coming to the marriage feast.

It is easy to have regular but very superficial relationships with God just as we can with people. Meeting a person several times a day and saying 'hallo' and commenting on the weather won't help us to know anyone except in a very superficial way. Sometimes perhaps we may think that developing a closer relationship will take up time and involve us when we are busy or occupied with things and people who interest us more. Quite often too, I believe, people are afraid, for one reason and another, to develop a relationship with God. They are prepared to have a nodding acquaintance with him and will say a few prayers when it suits them or when they want something. But we are afraid of a deeper and more regular relationship; we are afraid that he will change us, though we may not really believe that he could, but then again, he might! We are afraid perhaps of letting the Holy Spirit act in us, or of discovering our faults or our emptiness. In personal relationships too, I think, we are often afraid of letting another person too much into our lives because we realise that getting to know and love people can bring pain as well as great joy. Also we are afraid that others will see us as we really are, without any of the pretences we put up before the world. But God knows exactly what we are like and what we think and feel, and he still continues to love us. This is true, and this we have to believe, and so with him we can and should be as we are, without any pretence.

Also when we pray, we should learn to pray as whole persons. Perhaps as a result of interpreting medieval spiritual writers wrongly, there has been a tendency to see prayer as something only concerned with the so-called spiritual part of man. Medieval writers seemed to regard man as a group of separate faculties, each of which approached God independently and in a different manner. This was their way of trying to clarify and make things clearer for their readers who understood their approach though it is foreign to us today. It was also, however, partly due to the tidy, rather legal approach of the Latin mind which liked things neatly compartmented. The Greek fathers tended to have a rather more all-over view of man. For the Western spiritual writers the division was usually the intellect, the will and memory, and the body was often discounted or seen as something which had to be tamed and kept in check. Now we regard man much more as a whole. Thinking, feeling and willing are recognized as being inter-connected in every activity or mental process. Also man is accepted as not being exclusively rational; he is regarded as being intuitive, a creature of instinct with a subconscious about which we know remarkably little. God's grace and love affects the whole of us, both body and soul and this includes the subconscious. The body is not the enemy of the spirit but the normal channel through which it expresses itself.

In human relationships it is no use being stand-offish, and shut in; there has to be some going out to meet the other. There has to be an attempt at *rapport*. This is true with prayer, the self-giving of as much as possible of ourselves at any given time is essential as I have mentioned. We cannot simply pray with the parts of us that we regard as spiritual; the whole of us, hearts, minds, emotions, intuitions, instincts and bodies have to be taken into prayer. We have to pray 'total', Christ would seem to have prayed with his whole being; the bloody sweat in the garden shows us plainly how his body was in it.

We have to put our heart into our relationships if they are to be real and worthwhile. The Hebrews regarded the heart as the centre of the unity of man and for them it was the seat and centre of life. It could denote the inward man, or could be used to describe the whole being of a person. The heart was not just the seat of emotion and of the tenderer affections, but also, for example, of fortitude and courage. It was the seat of the will, of the intention, which is so important in prayer, for out of the heart, we read in the Old Testament and the New, proceeds thoughts good and ill, and also it can be either faithful or perverse. From the heart comes a love-knowledge that is the response of the whole man to the reality of the world, of other men and of God. In the New Covenant proclaimed by Jeremiah the Lord says he will put his law within his people and write it upon their hearts so that they will all know him (Jer. 31 33). So it is that the heart is regarded as the inmost core of our being, or as later spiritual writers were to say the peak or apex of our soul, and it is where God meets us.

Our relationship with God should, therefore, be involved with our heart as representing the centre and unity of our being. Our response to him has to affect our will which, as it were, has its origin in the heart and makes us tend towards him in love, and draw as much of our being as possible into relationship with him. So this unity includes our wills, our thinking faculties, our emotions, instincts, bodies – the lot.

Our minds are important when we relate to God. We have to think about, read and hear about him too. But it is not enough just to know about him with our minds; we must also experience him. It is comparatively easy to read about prayer and to be quite knowledgeable about the theory of it without having any experience of God. Many people know the Christian message with their minds but never let it touch them and their hearts. It is rather like giving a man a cookery book and telling him to learn how to make an omelette. He may say he knows all about it, but until he experiments and tries making omelettes, he will only know theoretically. We can be like this with prayer and relating to God. We can make it a mental exercise without experiencing the relationship and without letting it touch our hearts and our lives.

Emotions, feelings, and instincts come into our

relationship with God. Though I have talked about the importance of the will in love, I do not want to minimise the part emotion and feeling play in relating to God. Feelings certainly come into play when we relate to people. There is in the Psalms a wide range of feeling about life, about people and about the Lord; feelings are certainly important to the Psalmist! The stiff upper lip, British approach, never showing any emotion, is not necessarily a good thing in prayer! Anyway it seems to be much less part of the British character than formerly. People show emotion and feelings in public; they hold hands, embrace and kiss quite openly in front of others, and do not seem embarrassed. We appear to be less ashamed to show emotion than before. Probably, until recently too, there was a tendency to down-grade emotions in prayer.

Often in the past prayer has been too exclusively connected with our thought processes, and not nearly enough room has been allowed to feelings. After all if God is love, we must surely respond in love with all its wide range of emotions and attitudes. Weeping, for example, in some spiritual traditions is part of prayer. Certain people were said to have the 'gift of tears'. They weep in sorrow for their sins or the sins of the world, or both. Saint Dominic and Saint Ignatius Lloyola both wept a great deal and it was seemingly part of their relationship with God. I remember a Russian Orthodox friend of mine complaining that it was impossible to weep in a church in England, as someone would always come up and ask if she were all right. It was kind of people to be concerned but she wished to weep before the Lord in prayer. The woman in the gospel story who anointed Jesus' feet, washed them with her tears in Saint Luke's account of the story (Lk. 7.38). Also we can bubble with joy in prayer as we praise and thank God. Or we can be filled with an overwhelming love for him. All emotions are possible in prayer, but if they are not there we must not worry and try to manufacture them. We must pray as we can and as we are when we come to prayer. If we are empty and bored, our relationship with God will have to begin from this emptiness and boredom. All aspects of our life can come into prayer. Also we should try to use the body to help us to pray, and not see it as a hindrance and try to ill-treat it so as to keep it still and in order. Most people find it helpful to be relaxed, and many nowadays find sitting the most natural way to pray. Position in prayer is something that is very personal, and people have to discover what suits them best. Kneeling is obviously right at some stages in our lives; we can be driven to our knees in adoration, or penitence. Some always find kneeling best, whilst others may stand, sit, even walk about. The Lotus position is popular too today, though those who are not double-jointed or young, may find it extremely unhelpful! People who pray in bed often find lying on the back is best, because it is less easy to go to sleep that way; and if you train yourself to pray this way you may ultimately find it impossible to go to sleep in this position as it becomes associated with prayer and being attentive to God. The hands seem important in prayer. They can be clasped together, or touch each other in some way or other, or can be outstretched with palms upward.

Position in prayer depends very much on the individual.

If you are a soldier, for example, kneeling upright or standing at attention before the Lord may be your correct position for prayer. However try to use the body as an aid to your prayer and as part of you when you are relating to God in private.

When we reach the state of being able to pray 'total', all our being will be in the relationship, probably either in a relaxed forgetting of self or by a concentration of all our faculties on God in love that is almost without feeling (the *Cloud of Unknowing's* 'naked intent') or in adoration, which in its most complete form, can be a forgetting of self. This however does not happen all at once. We have, when we first start praying more seriously, to communicate with God as best as we can, though as our relationship deepens we come to know him in every part of our being in a united way. God has given us a tongue, a mind, a heart, so we can talk to him, we can sing if we like singing, we can think of him and we can use our emotions or be silent with him. We can share all our joys and sorrows with him. At the start of a human relationship there is a lot of talking, later perhaps we think a great deal about the person concerned and this may grow into affection, and later the relationship may make possible affectionate companionable silence.

We are human and our relationship with God should affect our whole humanity, both body and spirit, our living and our praying. Look at Jesus as he lived on earth. He teaches how to pray not only through 'the Lord's prayer', but by going away alone to pray, by talking with his disciples, by living in companionship with them, and by giving them the example of his daily living. Remember, he called the twelve 'to be with him' (Mk. 3.14.) and still communicates with us through the things of ordinary life, through the breaking of bread for example. He shows us how to live in communion with the Father throughout life in all its ups and downs. And even dying, he communicates to us how to pray in the suffering and in the agony of death, and then through coming alive again in the resurrection. And to help us to live in this continuous communication with the Father he gives us the Spirit and a new dimension or experience of him.

Our response to the Spirit too has a wide span and covers all our living from its heights to its depths; it will stretch from the extreme of a crude child-like demand to that of disinterested adoration, offered to 'God himself and none of his works'. At one end of the span we acknowledge the lowliness of our humanity, which is our creatureliness or createdness, and our utter dependence on the Spirit, and in doing this we turn to the Lord who can meet all our needs and recognise our need to be with Jesus. At the other end of the span our spirit adores and is captivated by the mysterious beauty of God in a disinterested, undemanding kind of way. Between these two extremes there is no point at which the intercourse of spirit with Spirit cannot take place.

We live our lives on a great variety of levels and our relationship to God can throughout any day be on an equal number of levels. Throughout all the wide range of man's living he can be closely in touch with God, both demanding from him and giving himself to him in adoration. We cannot live on the heights the whole time and often seem to spend most of our time on the

dull monotonous plains, but even here we are in communion with him if we let ourselves be, though
sometimes this communion can be as undefined and
seemingly as dull as the plains themselves.

Like all relationships, our relationship with God can
be exciting and wonderful and then at other times it is
something that needs working at and that requires effort
from us. He is always with us but we have to deepen our
perception of this, and grow in openness to his presence
and come to realise and know that we are living with
him throughout all the activities of our life. Our task is
to 'prepare the way of the Lord, and make straight his
paths' — that is we have to work at our relationship with
God, for his response to us generally comes along the
ways we have prepared. He reveals himself to us as we
stumblingly try to communicate with him. So we have,
at certain stages at any rate, to make a continued effort
in a disciplined way.

I believe for most people prayer is a combination of
discipline and spontaneity, and that at the start of getting
down to prayer one has to have a regular fixed time
when one withdraws to be with God. Secondly we must
develop what the spiritual writers have called 'the
practice of the presence of God'. This means that we try
to realise that God is always with us and learn how to
keep the relationship with him open. We have to practise
this awareness every day and so to develop a kind of
communion with God which is always there, or to put it
another way to develop a consciousness of God which is
never far from the surface of the mind. There are
various devices which can help at the start of this
practice, one of the most useful perhaps being short

prayers ejaculated throughout the day.

Christians of all denominations have experienced this sense of always living with God. It is not something just for saints, it is essential for ordinary sinners.

To conclude we have to learn to be ourselves with God in prayer, we have to pray from whatever situation we are in and not pretend that we are other than we are. It is no use building fantasies about ourselves and our situation in the presence of God. We have to pray with as much of our being as we can, mind, affection, will, body in as united a way as we can, and we have to accept God in the way he gives himself to us — whether it is in darkness, in light, in pain or in joy. And we have to let God into and allow him to touch all aspects of our life. I believe that life lived in touch with God is more real than any other way for one becomes one's self in a freer, more liberated way. It is demanding but very worthwhile.

Relating in Daily Life

There may not seem to be very many direct statements in the gospels about how our Lord prayed, but if the gospels are read attentively with eyes, ears and hearts open, we find hints and clues about his continual relationship with his Father and how he discovered and responded to his Father's will in all things. St. Luke's gospel, for example, shows how Jesus often went away alone to pray and suggests that he was always in touch with his Father in daily life, whilst St. John's gospel indicates Jesus' continuous closeness to the Father particularly in his prayer before his betrayal. There would seem to be in Jesus' life a twofold way of prayer; he had his times alone with his Father as well as keeping in touch with him throughout his daily life. There is no doubt that prayer was at the heart of Jesus' living. We also should have this twofold pattern of prayer, times alone with God, and the development of a sense of living all life in touch with him. Most of us have to work at developing our relationship with God in this double way which is rather like the way we relate to a friend we are fond of. We make time to be with them, and we also think of them or have them at the back of our minds during the day.

There is an apocryphal saying of Jesus, 'Cleave the

wood and you will find me; raise the stone and I am there'. I think this means that Jesus is there when the carpenter is working wood and the builder is building a wall. He is with us in our daily activities if we will recognise him, and this recognition should help us in our work, and encourage us in our worship and sense of his continual presence.

I want in this chapter to look at prayer in daily life for I believe it is very important for us to grow into a consciousness of living with God throughout the whole day and so to practise the presence of God in daily life. Brother Lawrence, a seventeenth century monk who spent most of his life working in the kitchen of his monastery wrote 'It is a great delusion to imagine that prayer-time should be different from any other, for we are equally bound to be united to God by work at work-time as by prayer as prayer-time.'[1] There are a number of ways of doing this but at the start praying as we go about our daily tasks is very helpful. You can pray about everything you do, either in set-prayers, or spontaneous prayers, or by having a verse from the Bible which you learn by heart and brood on throughout the day, or by saying from time to time the little arrow-prayers which I call short prayers.

The Gaelic people in the north of these islands use, or used to use, beautiful prayers when they began, or when they were performing certain tasks. There were, for example, prayers for getting up, for dressing, for washing, for lighting the fire, making beds, milking cows, making hay, setting out on a journey, going out in

1. *The Practice of the Presence of God,* ed. D. Attwater (Paraclete Books, London 1962).

a boat, lighting the lamps, and so on. I do not know any for washing up but there may have been one.[2]

The following prayer for the lighting of a fire is a good example of the Gaelic type;

> I will kindle my fire this morning
> In the presence of the holy angels of heaven.
> . . . . . .
> Without malice, without jealousy, without envy,
> Without fear, without terror of anyone under the sun,
> But the holy Son of God to shield me.
>
> God, kindle thou in my heart within
> A flame of love to my neighbour,
> To my foe, to my friend, to my kindred all.
> To the brave, to the knave, to the thrall,
> O Son of loveliest Mary,
> From the lowliest thing that liveth,
> To the name that is highest of all.[1]

This prayer gives kindling a wider context and significance than the actual action, in that it sees the fire as being symbolic of the flame of love which we should have in our hearts for all the family of mankind and not only for our nearest and dearest, and there is usually in these prayers the sense of the closeness of God and of angels and saints to all living on earth as well as a respect for all God's creation. They recognize no division between the sacred and the secular for God, the Creator,

---

2. These prayers are quoted from *The Sun Dances,* collected by Alexander Carmichael, Edinburgh, 1954.
   See also the excellent little collection by Martin Reith which is called *God in our midst,* London, 1975.

is lovingly concerned with all aspects of life.

The following prayer to be said when a person is getting dressed shows that the outer action can have a deeper significance if one lives with a sense of the nearness of God;

> O Great God, aid Thou my soul
>> with the aiding of Thine own mercy;
> Even as I clothe my body with wool,
>> Cover Thou my soul with the shadow of Thy wing.

If we pray in this sort of way when we get dressed, we greatly enrich our lives and deepen our relationship with God. The Gaelic prayers frequently stress the presence of the Three Persons of the Trinity, as for example in the following washing or bathing prayer. 'Palmfuls' refer to the water that is cupped in the hands and then poured or splashed over the face and so on.

> The three palmfuls
> Of the secret Three
> To preserve thee
> From every envy
> Evil eye and death;
> The palmful of the God of Life,
> The palmful of the Christ of Love,
> The palmful of the Spirit of Peace,
> Triune
> Of Grace.

Most of life seems to have been covered by specific prayers, which usually start with a specific situation and connect it with God in a wider way. The words used in these prayers may not be quite the kind we would use today, though they have a strength and lack of sentimentality which gives them a timeless appeal. Any prayers which do link daily tasks with God in some specific way or other can help to increase the sense of his presence in our lives. So you may find it helpful either to learn set prayers that connect with occupations or to invent your own spontaneous ones as you go through the day. Also some people have prayers pinned up in certain places in the home such as, for example, over the sink so that they can read and say them as they wash up.

Some learn a verse of the Bible each month or each week, and as I have indicated, live with it and use it throughout the day at the sort of points of time which I am going to suggest that short prayers can be employed. Any prayer-verse learnt can be prayed with the lips, or interiorly and mentally, or with the heart. For example a verse like the following from a hymn by George Herbert could be said at the beginning of any task:

'Teach me my God and King,
In all things thee to see:
And what I do in anything
To do it unto thee.'

I want now to consider the use of short prayers in some detail, keeping in mind that any of the suggested ways of praying in daily life can be used at the times mentioned for short prayers.

Short prayers can be employed in all stages of the spiritual life, and are possible in most circumstances for the majority of people. They have firm gospel backing. Jesus always responded to the short requests made to him in faith ('Lord save us we perish',

Matt. 8.25; Peter's 'Lord save me', Matt. 14.30), to the prayer of the man born blind ('Jesus, thou son of David, have mercy on me', Mk. 10.47), and to others who made demands in a similar way. This kind of prayer was not limited to petition, but could express love and adoration as Thomas did when he said 'My Lord and my God'. The very shortness of the prayer can so forcibly embody our need and love.

Short prayers were, and are still important in the Jewish tradition. The early Christians too used phrases like *Maranatha* ('Lord come quickly') and *'Hallelujah'* ('Praise the Lord'). Monks of the Eastern Church often prayed short phrases from the Bible almost continually. The anonymous English fourteenth century, medieval writer of *The Cloud of Unknowing* advocated the use of short prayers, often only a little word, because a 'short prayer pierceth heaven'. Later, in the seventeenth century, Thomas Ken, a saintly non-juring Anglican bishop, suggested that the uninstructed in his diocese of Wells should use 'short prayers, little more than brief ejaculations, easily learnt, remembered and understood' and this advice still holds good for today.

Short prayers can, perhaps, be used in two main ways in daily life, besides forming for some the basis for times of set prayer. Firstly, we can address remarks to God about what is happening to us more or less spontaneously throughout the day, and secondly, we can use short phrases which can be repeated at certain fixed times in order to make us aware of God's presence and to deepen the sense of this perception.

The first kind of short prayer can be used when things happen to us that make us happy, glad, sad, sorrowful, infuriated, hurt physically or wounded mentally, or when we are otherwise distressed. It is very easy to pray to God when we are in trouble; even people who do not think they believe in God, may utter a short prayer in times of crisis. Fewer people thank God for the good things which we are given. Remember how often Jesus said 'Father, I thank you ...' We should make an effort to thank God in a few short words for the beauty, joy, goodness of a person, event, or thing, or when things have gone well. There is so much beauty and goodness we take for granted, and by doing this we lose the sense of gratitude and can become grudging in our appreciation of things and people and deaden our awareness of the wonderful, and so miss much joy. There is so much in life that we should be thankful for, and if we are open and grateful, life can become fuller and more meaningful.

We should especially express thanks to God for the kind of experience of beauty that takes our breath away and makes us forget ourselves by the wonder of it, whether it be of music, nature, poetry, people, art — when we have as it were, been surprised by joy. Such phrases as 'Lord, you are wonderful', 'I thank you', or 'Lord, it's wonderful', or simply 'thank you', or 'praise God', or 'I love you, Lord' can be employed. Use what seems natural to you and suits you, and not a pious platitude which you feel is the right thing to say. If we keep remembering to thank God for the small joys of life, it should become second nature for us to do so, and when more wonderful experiences come we may be able to extend our thankfulness into deep adoration. If we learn to prolong the feeling of thankfulness, a growing sense of gratitude to God can come to underlie all our daily living and help to deepen our prayer and our sense of dependence on him.

Short prayers can be a wonderful spring-board to greater love of God and knowledge of ourselves. If we develop a sense of gratitude and thankfulness in daily life, thanksgiving in our set times of prayer becomes less mechanical and less of a chore. It may even make it easier to say a spontaneous thanks to God at night as we drop exhausted into bed!

In sorrow, in fear, distress or danger, as I have already said, we are more inclined to rush to God with cries for help. Some people, however, feel ashamed because it is in these circumstances they turn most to God, and feel that this is taking advantage of him. But as at these times we are more open since our guard is down and we are more ourselves, God can reach us and touch us in a deeper way than we realise. There is no need to feel ashamed. Prayers such as 'Lord, help me' (the prayer of the Syro-Phoenician woman Mt.15. 25); 'I can't do anything myself', 'Save me', 'Keep me safe', or just 'Lord' which come almost unthinkingly to our lips or minds, or hearts, can be very deep prayers. Also phrases based on words of Scripture in which God is the speaker can be very strengthening. For example 'Fear thou not for I am with you' or 'Peace be still' which was said by Jesus can be most comforting. Such prayers help to awaken our sense of dependence on God.

Sometimes too when we are in great pain, or utterly exhausted or seemingly without the capacity to think very much, all we can say is 'Give me strength', 'Keep me going', 'Don't leave me', 'Into thy hands', or just 'help', or again 'Lord' almost as a sigh, or 'Jesus – mercy'. Such short prayers can sustain and support us when everything else seems useless. It is a kind of letting go into God, a handing over to him, and can lead to a wonderful trust and dependence on him. It is a putting of our hands 'in the hands of the Man from Galilee'. Again as with the times of gratitude, we can, when we have come through the exhausted and suffering situation, continue this sense of dependence either by keeping on saying short prayers or by letting the sense of dependence underlie and undergird our living and breathing. Usually when we are helpless through exhaustion or pain, we have to let others help us in a way which our self-dependence will not generally let us do. It is good if we can prolong this sense of dependence on others as it helps us to be humble and to appreciate in a real way our inter-connectedness with each other. Humility is, after all, just the acceptance of the reality of ourselves as we are and of the fact that we are all dependent on God and each other.

Short prayers are useful too, in the night, when one cannot sleep, and their repetition can be more helpful than the counting of sheep! The gentle rhythm of the prayer repeated over and over again can soothe and still an over-active mind. Also short prayers can be used when one is attacked by temptations to lose one's temper ('Lord, still me, calm me'), by uncharitable thoughts ('Get thee behind me, Satan', 'help, Lord'), by jealousy ('Lord, help'; 'stop me, Lord'), unclean thoughts ('Jesus save me') and so on.

Again, when our work or our lives are apparently senseless and frustrating, or when people seem utterly impossible 'Lord give me strength', 'Lord help me to understand', 'Help me to see you there', 'Lord, give me patience' can encourage one to go on. You can say them once, or keep repeating them to yourself over and over again until your tension or difficulty is eased. Sometimes repetition of such prayers is the only thing that stops one from shouting at the difficult person who keeps on and on saying the same thing, relating the same trouble or the long-winded tale of their youth. Whatever way you pray in these frustrating situations about the people, who make you impatient or nearly drive you out of your mind, you will bring God in, and you will share your problem, and theirs, with him. By doing this we can become more considerate and open to the problems of others and perhaps draw them into our sense of living in touch with God.

We can, of course, pray in shorter or longer ways for the people we meet in the course of the day, either for those we come into close contact with in work or at home or for those we pass by in the street or shop, the old man who can scarcely walk, the lame, the crippled, the person over-loaded with shopping bags, the tense, the sad or unsmiling person. We can quite simply say 'Lord, help them' or 'Lord, strengthen them', 'Make them happy' or whatever seems to be needed for them. This kind of approach, too, can make us aware of people and their needs and help us to grow compassionate and understanding of others. Again we can say a thankful prayer when we see a happy person or when we learn of someone's good fortune.

The kind of prayers which I have been discussing, arise more or less spontaneously out of situations we find ourselves in. The *second* kind which I want to consider, we make ourselves do at certain fixed times. If our occupations are divided by hours, or fixed divisions of time, say a prayer when the hour begins or ends; if you are a teacher or pupil, you can do this as you go from one class to another; if you are a secretary, when you go in and out of your boss's office; if you are doing house-work such as cleaning and cooking, you can pray when you begin or end a certain task. If you are interviewing people, you can go about it in the same sort of way, praying at the beginning or end of session. Or some people pray when they go up and down stairs, or when they hear a clock strike, or when they go in and out of a door. This may seem rather a mechanical way of keeping in touch with God, but quite often when we are learning to keep turned to him, we tend to forget, if we do not use a certain amount of discipline. Discipline and regularity are needed in any form of activity or occupation in which we hope to grow and develop. For example, when you are learning to drive a car, you have to make yourself do certain things, such as looking in the mirror to see what is behind you, but when you become an experienced driver you do it without any conscious thought. It becomes second nature to you. Something like this can happen with prayer as you become more practised in it; and devices for remembering cease to be needed.

Prayers at the beginning and end of the day should form part of this kind of framework. It is essential that at the beginning of the day, we commend ourselves to God. By doing this we give God a priority over all other things, worries, plans, temptations, the lot. Some-thing short can be said, perhaps 'Here I am, Lord; I love you; help me to do your will in all things today', or more formally 'Lord of my life, God of my salvation, I offer you this coming day; I want in all things to do your will'. It is helpful to keep to the same phrases so that they become part of the routine of your life. You can also ask for grace for yourself and add sentences of intercession for others. None of this need take very long, but it can give you a sense of using the day for God. Similarly a short phrase or two can be said at night to commend ourselves into the hands of God before sleep.

A feature of life today despite all its rush and hurry, is that we spend quite a lot of time waiting. We wait for buses, trains, planes, lifts, in traffic jams or at traffic lights. Praying can prevent us from feeling frustrated and angry at having to wait when we want to be getting on! Again we spend quite a lot of time going from place to place, either walking, biking, motoring, or going by train, sea, air or water. These, too, are times when we can repeat short prayers or pray in other ways. Motoring can be very good for praying, especially if we are alone, or with someone we know well and do not feel obliged to keep up a conversation with.

There are also many hours in the day when we are engaged in occupations when it is immaterial whether we think of one thing or another. Some tasks only need a surface concentration, such as housework, some cooking, feeding the baby, knitting, sewing, cleaning the car, having a bath, gardening, waiting for customers to make up their minds and so on. We often daydream then or do not think much about anything, and we can, with benefit, give these times to conscious prayer. Some people instead of using short prayers, pray for others at such times, or ponder on a phrase from Scripture or a verse from a hymn. For others short prayers may be better. If we do persist in using them, short prayers can come to weave a pattern into our life, so that something imposed on an unwilling nature becomes natural and unforced.

I will try and show how these prayers can be employed. The choice of short prayer or phrase that we say in times of waiting, or when our minds are not fully engaged with our occupations, or at the times we set for them, will vary with each individual. One phrase can be used the whole time as Christians in the Eastern Orthodox tradition do, or the phrase can be changed according to one's situation or mood. Cassian, a fifth century Western monk, much influenced by the fathers of the Eastern church, advocated the recital of the opening words of Psalm 70, 'O God, make speed to save me, O Lord, make haste to help me'; a certain Saint Joanniky used to repeat 'The Father is my hope, the Son is my refuge, the Holy Spirit is my protection'; and the most loved prayer of the Orthodox church, the Jesus prayer, is 'Lord Jesus Christ, Son of God, have mercy on me, a sinner'.[3] This is based on the publican's prayer and is used in shorter or longer forms. Other phrases from the Bible can equally well be chosen though those containing the name of Jesus or the Persons of the Trinity seem to be the best loved.

Prayers using the name of Jesus alone or in one or other forms of the Jesus prayer have a long tradition.

3. See Archimandrite Kallistos Ware, *The Power of the Name*, Fairacres Publication, 1974. This gives an excellent account of the ways the Jesus prayer can be used.

Saint Peter in the *Acts of the Apostles* (4.12) said we can only be saved by the name of Jesus Christ, and did not Jesus say that we should pray in his name 'if you ask anything of the Father, he will give it to you in my name' (John 16.23)? He, himself, prays in the prayer he gave us 'Hallowed be thy name'. The disciples perform miracles in his name, that is by using his power (Mark 9.39) and baptise in it (1 Cor 6.11). In biblical times a person's name was regarded as almost synonymous with his being and character. In the Old Testament to invoke God's name is to put oneself before him and in his presence, in a kind of self-offering, and because of the close relation between name and person, the name of Jesus is used in the New Testament as synonymous with Jesus himself, denoting his character and authority. The name of Jesus used as a prayer is a sign of his presence with us as a protector, guide, comforter, and as someone to be loved and adored as a friend and brother. Self-offering comes into it too. There are very many ways the name can be prayed. Saint Patrick's Breastplate 'I bind unto myself today the strong name of the Trinity' suggests that the name of the Trinity can be used in a similar way, as can 'Abba, Father'.

The prayer of the name used in the Far East seems to be somewhat similar to the Jesus prayer. 'Shiva' and 'Rama', names for the Divinity, are said as prayers by Hindus. 'Om' is regarded as the highest prayer of the name, and is considered to be the first word said by God when he reveals himself in creation or to individuals.[4]

---

4. See *Prayer* by the French Benedictine, Abhishiktananda, who lives in India, S.P.C.K. He gives an excellent account of the prayer of the name.

Abhishiktananda believes 'Abba, Father' is the Christian equivalent of Om as it was prayed by Jesus. 'It was his last prayer in Gethsemane and his last word on the Cross. Is this not an invitation to make the invocation 'Abba Father' the centre of our lives'?

The prayer of the name or the short prayer which can be repeated continuously can be said either with the lips, or in the mind, or in the heart, though none of these ways exclude the others. When the prayer is repeated simply with the lips, the mind may be distracted, but this does not matter, if the person praying repeats the name or phrase with respect and longing for the grace of God or with the intention of this longing. In the next stage, the prayer is prayed with the mind, that is with a simple mental awareness of it. In the third stage, the name is prayed in the heart, and the lips and mind do not operate. The prayer is, as it were, in the centre of one's being, and all desires are summed up in the one desire for God. The prayer may get taken into the rhythm of our breathing or somehow get linked with the beating of our heart. The whole of our being gets involved with the prayer, which seems to be connected with turning inwards into oneself. Phrases like 'the journey inwards' can be used to describe it. If such a method of prayer is employed it is wise to have a guide or friend to help.[5]

Some medieval writers, who advocated short prayers, appear to suggest instead of going inwards they help us to go out to God, though they lead ultimately to a similar stillness and unity of being. Some of these medieval writers who favoured short prayers, stressed their power to awaken and stimulate love of God, whilst

5. See K. Ware in the booklet just mentioned, p. 5.

others laid more emphasis on their use for strengthening the will in its pursuit of God. The first kind of prayer, frequently called affective (based on affectionate love) suggested the use of such phrases as 'God, I would love you more', 'help me to love you more perfectly' or sentences from the *Song of Songs*. These short, loving prayers which were called aspirations could almost be sighed. This kind of prayer, it was thought, would stimulate our love for God, and the more we pray in order to love God, the more God draws us to himself.

Some people consider this approach too emotional and for them the short prayer will be stretching out to God summed up in one short word, such as 'God', 'Jesus', 'Help', as suggested by the author of *The Cloud of Unknowing*. Such a simple word, which need not be repeated rhythmically like the prayer of the name, can embody the strong intention to reach God and can help to make God and his will the end of all our action in prayer and in life. This is so because the short phrase frequently repeated with the intention of keeping us alert to God's presence may be prayed with our surface mind at first, but can come to be prayed with our whole being until it becomes as natural as breathing. Like breathing, it becomes so much a part of us that we take it for granted. It can, as I have suggested, give us deep stillness and peace that continues throughout the day like a kind of background music which assures us of God's continual presence in daily life.

These kinds of prayers do not provide a technique or short cut to God, and must not be separated from the rest of our Christian life. The intention of loving God and of attaining to him must be accompanied by a desire to live for God and to do his will in all aspects of life.

The usefulness of ejaculatory prayer in its various forms continues throughout life with its many stages of spiritual growth. It can be of help when other kinds of prayers go dead on one or become impossible, and it can also express the highest kind of love and adoration. For example, Saint Francis of Assisi spent a whole night simply repeating over and over again 'My Lord and my God'. No longer phrase could express for him such intensity of adoration at that time. It is a very helpful way of prayer for those who lead busy lives and who wish to live and work with the sense of the presence of God always with them. And perhaps for some who have an undefined and unsatisfied longing, this kind of short prayer may stimulate love of God and lead them to the fulfilment of their unfulfilled desires.

But as I have suggested there are other ways of praying which can help people to come to live their lives with a sense of being in touch with God and each person has to discover which is God's way for him or her. The ways may vary as our lives change. When we come to relate more deeply to God, set prayers or phrases may become almost unnecessary, though, even when one has come to a close relationship with another person and live most our lives with a sense of their presence, we may find ourself murmuring the name of the beloved and this can happen in a deeper relationship with God.

Relating in Prayer Time

In the last chapter I suggested ways we could use to keep ourselves aware of living our daily life in touch with God who is always in touch with us. Here I want primarily to set out a simple scheme for the daily times of prayer when we go to be alone with God, or as alone as we can get. It is often very difficult to get away to be alone, and perhaps the bath may be the only place that we can find. Sometimes one may have to hide behind a newspaper, or pretend to write a letter in the family living-room, and this is not at all easy. If one can retreat into one's own room and shut the door as Jesus suggested, this is wonderful and what we should do, or to slip into a church whilst shopping or in the lunch hour, is good too.

People have to be ingenious in this crowded world we live in to find places and time for prayer. Usually where there is a will, a way can be found. For many the early morning is the ideal time, but having to rush off to work, or to get breakfast for the family makes this time impossible for a great number of people. In the evening many seem too tired and exhausted to pray for any length of time or at any depth. We have, however, to try and find time for prayer, and most people can, except, perhaps, the mother with a large family. She will have to make the most of her moments of waiting as was suggested in the last chapter, and grow into living in touch with God as she goes through the day. However, if say once a week or even once a month, she can manage to get away to be alone with God for several hours, this will help to deepen and strengthen her daily living with God. I know not every mother can manage this, but it is well worth trying to achieve. It is helpful for everyone to have a time by themselves humanly and physically speaking, as well as spiritually.

The way we pray when we go to be alone with God will vary according to our up-bringing, and Christian tradition. I have already tried to suggest that we should pray honestly and as we are, realising that God is always with us helping us to pray. Some Christian traditions suggest that we should pray in our own words about what we feel and as we feel at the time of praying, and others rely on more formal prayers which suit them and which they make their own. Many people find it helpful to learn some prayers by heart as this makes the understanding of the meaning of their content easier when they pray them; others find it useful to learn verses of the Bible or verses of hymns. These can help to stimulate their own prayers.

Whatever tradition we belong to, there is no doubt that at certain times when we are moved by love of God or for others, or by joy, need or sorrow we pray spontaneously and are very much aware of being in communion with him, and are alive to his response to us. But for many people these times of awareness and sense of close relationship to God are not continuous, and for some are even rare. We are all different and God calls us in many ways. We each have to learn to be open to the Spirit who helps us every time we pray, and to follow the way he is leading us personally. We must not be disheartened if he leads us in different and, perhaps, less spectacular ways than he does others. The aim of prayer is to bring us to greater knowledge and love of God, and as a result to produce in our lives such fruits of the Spirit as love, joy, peace, patience, kindness, goodness, faithfulness, gentleness and self-control (Gal.5.22).

When our impulse to pray is not strong, or when we cannot believe the Spirit is really helping us, our thoughts are more likely to wander, it is then useful to have a planned way of praying, a kind of framework into which we fit our prayers. We must not worry if we lose the sense of God with us and only have an awareness of absence. The Spirit is as unpredictable as the gale-force winds that blow in all directions on islands, and God is transcendent and his ways are beyond our understanding.

A planned way of praying can help us not only to keep at it, but can also aid us in widening and deepening the content of our prayer, though the liturgical prayer of the church does this too. When we are moved to pray through stress or emotion, prayer can be limited in range and often concerned only with ourselves and so needs to be combined with a wider, if less intense approach.

It is a good thing, for example, to extend our thanksgiving and prayers for others beyond ourselves and our immediate concerns; this both expands our view and takes our minds away from ourselves. Also it is important to develop a habit of prayer which can be a support to us when prayer goes dry or seemingly dead.

So it is helpful for many in their set prayer-time to

follow a pattern that is independent of moods or experiences though these will naturally come into it. Even in great distress, for example, we should make room for thanksgiving, and in joy remember the sorrows of the world and take them into our prayer. The pattern or plan will provide a definite sequence whatever our mood.

The following is a suggested plan[1] for set times of prayer which can vary in length from ten minutes to half an hour or more.

1. Shut the mind to other activities, interests and attractions.
2. Regard God with reverence and adoration.
3. Think of the things you want to bring to him and
4. Speak of these.
5. Accept God's response.
6. Withdraw reverently from this time of prayer.

I will try and explain how this scheme works. It will, of course, not suit everyone. At first, probably the elements mentioned will have to be performed deliberately; later they may become the natural way of acting.

1. Go to your usual place of prayer and kneel, sit, stand or whatever attitude you find conducive to prayer. If the place is fairly public, a simple and unobtrusive gesture such as clasping the hands may be the only way of indicating to ourselves that we are about to pray. A ceremonial gesture is helpful, however small it may be.

Christ says 'enter into your room and shut the door', so withdraw your mind from anything that is not God.

1. I am indebted to George Stewart's *The Lower Levels of Prayer*, (Edinburgh, 1969) for this approach and plan.

Drop everything and relax. This withdrawal of the mind should be not so much an effort as a purpose or intention. If it is made an effort, it is self-defeating, for the mind becomes absorbed in the effort. Let the will to shut the world out be there; let a moment or two pass. This purpose and attitude will help to form a habit that should assist in closing the door on intrusion.

The Greek fathers stressed the necessity for the unification of one's self and for unity with God, and their idea that our being is torn in various directions and fragmented and that growth in union with Christ helps to bring the dissipated elements of our being into a wholeness and unity, is important when we pray. There is no doubt that when we come to pray, we experience very plainly how our minds and imaginations are drawn in a great number of directions. There are bound to be distractions but these matter much less than we think.

In the past, rightly or wrongly, ruthless renunciations of the world, of human relationships and even family duty were thought by some to be the way to get rid of interior distractions. Today, I believe, we must prepare ourselves to pray, not by ruthless renunciations but rather through living in a relaxed and deeply peaceful way in the atmosphere of God the whole time, and by trying to avoid things that divide our attention and fragment our being, as for example, superficial T.V. programmes that jump from topic to topic and never touch us deeply. Constant triviality or snippetery as it is sometimes called, can be more of a hindrance to prayer than we realise. Activities which concentrate our being and help us to unite our intentions can be remote preparation for prayer-time. A great many of man's psychological problems today may well stem from lack of purpose.

So when we come to prayer we should have the intention of praying because it is God's will for us, yet we must not make great efforts at concentration, but rather try to have the purpose and intention of dropping everything that seems to separate us from God. Somehow attention and relaxation have to be combined. John V. Taylor writes 'true attention is an involuntary self-surrender to the object of attention. The child who is absorbed is utterly relaxed.' There is no doubt the way we live out of prayer-time affects our prayer; if we apply ourselves to our daily activities, our habit of attention will help our prayer.

It is, therefore, important to develop a relaxed attention as well as a stillness in one's self. Yet somehow when one tries to do this in prayer-time, one can get very fidgety. A relaxed bodily position can be a great help. Also rhythmical breathing can assist some people to still themselves and become mentally calm, and so make them more open to God. Being quiet and relaxed in the atmosphere of God is an important part of prayer. If we are very wrapt up in ourselves or too preoccupied with others we can be very tense. Attention to something and tenseness are very different. Each person has to find the best way of growing into relaxed attention at the beginning of prayer. Developing a sense of living all day in the presence of God is an excellent preparation too.

2. To return to the suggested scheme of prayer, the *second* thing is to look at God with reverence and adoration. The Lord's prayer starts with adoration, and

wonder at the holiness of God: God in his glory and then man and his needs is the order of this prayer. We would much rather start with us and our needs. But this was not Jesus' way. I believe this starting with God is of the greatest importance, though it may go against the grain for us. Jesus says 'the pure in heart shall see God', and so the vision of God should be the aim of every Christian. We must be still and know that he is God, that is, we must forget ourselves in the self-forgetting wonder and love which leads to purity of heart. He is always with us, but in prayer time we should make a definite effort of will to realise this and so deepen our perception of his presence.

Think, perhaps, of God's love, holiness, his glory and say a word or phrase like 'Holy, holy, holy, Lord God Almighty' or it is of the greatest value to look at Jesus. For, as Kenneth Kirk says, 'Jesus gave a vision of God where others could only speak of it'. Consider an aspect of the revelation of God in Jesus Christ. Think perhaps of the healing Christ, the Christ who calms the storms, the patient Christ, the crucified Christ, the transfigured and risen Christ. Look at any such revelation, slowly say a phrase, or mull over a thought about God, looking at God as it were. When you do this, have in your mind 'It is to you I come, my God, my very God'. The wonder and glory of adoration may catch you, or the peace of God enfold you and you will be entranced by the beauty of holiness. Even if this does not happen, you will always pray with a deepening consciousness of God being with you, though quite often you may feel that you have not been really praying. We have to come to realise that however we may feel, he is eternally there.

We are sure of him whether we are in darkness or light so we give thanks for his great glory and holiness.

3. and 4. Thinking and speaking interiorly about what we want to put before God go together and often interpenetrate. You will probably want to include in your prayer thanksgiving, confession, intercession, petition and you will have to follow whichever order seems most helpful or natural to you. But whatever act you are intending, think about it first. The actual prayer will often be far deeper than the thought, for prayer awakens and extends every thought and desire, but it is helpful to begin with quiet consideration. The latter is a 'preparing the way of the Lord' for it provides him with a way to take us beyond the desire we began with, if we let him.

If you, for example, start with thanksgiving, consider what is your particular thanksgiving for the day, or if you use a book of prayers ponder the clauses so that they come alive for you and become your own prayer. After thinking, express your thanks, coldly if your heart is not warm, courteously if this is all you can manage, but at least have the intention of thanking God however empty you feel. Sometimes your thankfulness will be so deep that it is impossible to put it in words. Note that in this kind of prayer the mind, heart and will all play some part, and when we are with God wordlessly, the whole of us is concentrated on him and we are praying 'total'. Thanksgiving is very important for so often we take the wonderful things of life for granted as well as our daily bread, and the love and affection of others and of God. We should keep remembering to thank until it becomes second nature to live in thankfulness to God.

Petition may follow next. Again first think of the needs that you want to put before God, and then lay them before him in trust and openness. God will respond in some way; perhaps in some surprising way, perhaps in the ordinary events of life, or by changing your attitude or approach. The important thing is to develop one's relationship with God so that all your desires and problems are put before him. God purifies our desires if we approach him honestly. By holding back any desire, whether good or bad, we shut him out of the situation, and afford him no opportunity for freeing us from wrong or misguided longings for ourselves or others.

Intercession may come next, following the same kind of pattern, thought first and then the formulation of the prayers.

Confession for many will follow on after adoration, for having looked at the greatness and purity of God, we may be driven to recognise our smallness and imperfection, but it can equally well come at the end of our prayer and form part of our response to God. When we confess, we should face and acknowledge our sins to ourselves, and when we have done this confess them to God and believe that he is more ready to forgive than we are to confess, cast your cares on him and accept that he forgives and delivers you from your sin. And ask him to help you avoid doing the same sort of thing again. Most of us know when we have offended against God or against our neighbour though for many, however, nowadays a sense of sinfulness only comes late in the life of prayer, when we grow closer to God and see our lives in the light of his holiness.

5. Accepting God's response. It is good to end prayer

time with an act of the will indicating a willingness to respond to God and to be open to his response to us. Like our Lord's mother we may say 'be it unto me according to thy will', or like Jesus in Gethsemane where he said 'this is what I would like, but, Father, as you will'. God can respond through our will which accepts his whether it is known or still unknown.

6. A reverent ending helps though it is not essential for the prayer. Outwardly it consists of finishing your prayer, spending a minute or two in stillness, then leaving the place of prayer. A slow, gentle withdrawal has a calming effect on the numerous other interests that are ready to rush into the mind. In this way you go out into life carrying an atmosphere of peace with you and a sense of God's closeness though you may often be unaware of this, for though the prayer may have seemed featureless or even frustrating, God will have affected you in some deep way. If you keep on in faith God will become more and more a reality in your life, and you will begin to see him a little more clearly though perhaps only in a dark cloudy way.

The above is simply an example of a scheme of prayer, and there are many other ways of setting about it. However quite a number of people to whom I suggested this scheme have found it helpful.

I would like to stress two points which seem important to me. Firstly, if it is possible, have a regular time for being alone (or as alone as you can get) with God. Secondly, after you have set yourself ready to pray, start off by looking at God in some way and making yourself aware of his closeness to you. Books used to say put yourself in the presence of God, but as God is always with you, it is of more help to remember that it is you who have to respond and open yourself to him. Either read some verses of the Bible to make yourself aware of him, or look at a picture of Jesus, or hold a crucifix or do all these three things. Discover what awakens you to an .awareness of God. I myself would begin with adoration of God, remembering his great love for me and all creation. If you start with God, you will probably become less self-centred and less self-concerned. This is the way the prayer Jesus gave his disciples begins and surely we should follow the way he pointed?

Asking

In this book I am trying to indicate how prayer can help us to relate to God and lead us to love him more deeply, and since asking is so important in any relationship I want to look at this element of prayer early on. Most people when they begin to pray usually start by asking God for things. This is natural for this is the way we relate to others, and get to know each other, and by doing this we are helped to grow as people. There is nothing disreputable in asking though some writers on prayer can make this seem so. Asking forms part of our life as we know it. We find out about other people by asking and they do about us throughout all our lives.[1]

Babies demand of their parents by means of crying; later they use words to indicate what they want. At first it is usually things to meet their bodily needs, but most of all they want protection and love, and the giving of food and warmth is part of this. Later the child knows what to expect and how to ask of the parents in a more complex way though its needs may remain very much the same. Throughout our lives we continue to ask of

1. cf. M. Nédoncelle 'The nature and use of prayer' 1964, London. Most recent books on prayer have been influenced by Fr. Nédoncelle's approach as has this chapter of mine.

each other, first from parents and teachers, and as we grow up asking goes far beyond the limits of the family, and our motives become more complicated and mixed. All our lives we will be asking from people who have greater knowledge than we have and the range of those asked can extend from garage mechanics and plumbers to theologians and philosophers!

We spend much of our time asking from each other. For example when we speak, we are asking to be listened to. We may wrap up much of our asking in a polite way: 'Would you mind doing such and such?', 'Could you please tell me the way?', 'May I talk to you?'. It is not rude to ask it is simply part of life. If we do not ask we will be living in a kind of vacuum with no contact with others. We get to know about ourselves and others and life by asking.

We also come to know God by asking from him, and our wants when we start praying can be pretty basic rather like a baby's, but underlying our demands too is a need to be noticed, a need for protection and love though we may not recognise this. God is the one who listens and loves us, but we have to ask and then listen. We tend to forget that he is always *asking* us to love him, that is praying to us, and his sending his Son, the Word, into the world is a token of this asking. I believe that our Lord told us to keep on asking so that we could come to realise God's love and get to know him better so that 'we come to ask such things as will please him'.

Asking as I have said plays a more important part in human life than we often recognise. We relate to each other through it for asking constitutes an important element in communication. Self-development requires that we should petition others. In relating to others through asking we start with some presuppositions about the person we ask from and by further asking we learn more until our asking is very much predetermined by the character of the person we ask of. The child takes into consideration what it knows of its mother's character by the way it asks. With God too we start asking from our situation as we are and from what we know of God. We have to keep asking so as to get to know him and find out what he wants of us as well as getting to know him by reading the gospel and learning about the Jesus of revelation. We are told in the gospels to pray to receive the mind of God, and everything else will follow on from this: 'seek ye first the kingdom of God and his righteousness and all these things shall be yours as well' (Matt. 6,33).

We have, however, to ask in order to come to some knowledge of the mind of God, so as to be able 'to ask such things as shall please him', and to discover what the kingdom is. Our asking will vary according to our present relationship with God. At first we do not realise and some never come to realise, that our deepest desire is to have the mind of God, the kingdom, or whatever other way we try to express this deep craving that is in man. We have to find out what God wants of us by facing up to him and asking him questions. In this way we come to learn a little about God and his will for us. It is through the practice of prayer that we come to know what we should be asking for. Prayer is a kind of training or apprenticeship through which we learn. It can be a kind of wrestling with God, rather like Jacob's wrestling with the angel. Though we get hurt in the wrestling we learn from it and are strengthened by it.

We have, therefore, as I have said before, to start from where we are and ask for what we feel are our needs whether they be material or improvements in our character. Of course God knows our needs but he wants us to ask so that we are made capable of receiving his gifts. By prayer we develop this capacity. We have to ask in honesty and ask for what we want, even if we are not sure whether we should. Our need gives God the opportunity to respond and influence us. When we are at our most helpless, he can influence us most. Jesus could not respond to the Pharisees who had no needs. We have to accept that God acts in the relationship of prayer. We look at him and ask from him and then we have to wait upon him. We have to learn to wait attentively. This is a part of petitioning which tends to get forgotten. We actively want to be doing the talking ourselves though it is most important for us to learn to wait on God so as to know what he wants of us and what *he wants us to want,* and for the strength and love to ask for this. Also in this waiting upon God we learn humility, and gradually come to perceive what we want is nothing less than God himself. No petitioner who tries to be open to God, can fail to have his horizon widened by asking, but if we ask with closed minds and do not listen, we are like the heathen whom our Lord condemns for babbling.

To give an example, when we ask for a sewing machine, a car, a new coat or something we think we need, ask and then stay quietly with God and in the light of his presence see how much you need it, what your motives are, think whether it will help you to be more efficient or whether you desire it through sheer possessiveness or to keep up with the neighbours. Ask God whether it will help you love him more and enable you to do his will better in the world. We should lay our needs before God like Hezekiah who put the letter containing the difficult demands of his enemies before God in the temple and then wait attentively as he did. We may for example ask God to make us recover quickly from an illness, but we should also ask, that if this is not to be, that we may be given patience and love so as to grow through it; to make it creative and not frustrating. Saint Catherine of Siena asked that through every event of her life, however frustrating and trying it might be that she should gain something from it. This should be our request too.

We read in John 15.7;

   'If you remain in me
   and my word remains in you
   you may ask what you will
   and you shall get it.'

but we have to grow in love of God and surrender to him before we reach this state! We generally begin our asking from ourselves, and not from our position in Christ, but through asking honestly and waiting on God, we can come to be so rooted and grounded in him that we will receive and the Holy Spirit will help us to ask aright.

Yet we have to go on asking in order to learn. We should ask as our Lord did in Gethsemane for something (in his case that the cup may pass) with the underlying presupposition that the Father's will is what matters. We have to keep on battering at God and yet trusting that what happens will be right. By doing this we can come to realise that what we want is God himself and not any lesser gift.

But we must be as we are and ask from him, day by day, simply and trustingly as a child. We cannot see what God's over-all economy is for us or for the world. We do not know what is good for us any more than a child does. Archbishop Anthony Bloom gives an excellent example of this. A boy sees his grandfather's false teeth in a glass and he prays that he may have teeth like this. He does not realise how much better off he is with his own teeth at the present time. Ultimately God may grant his request! We cannot know or understand God's timing. It is often part of his plan for us that we should wait for what we ask. Again it may be plain dangerous for us to get what we want until we are mature enough to use it. We are like young children who ask for matches to play with. They do not know the perils and dangers of the things they ask for, nor quite often do we.

We have to trust God, and keep on asking so that we may learn about him and his will for us. In some ways all prayer is petitioning. Our adoration is our response to God's asking for our love. We tend to forget that he asks from us too, and our praying and self-offering to him is our answer to him. Prayer is a continuous dialogue, a never ceasing wrestling match with God, and we have to keep on at it even if we do not see what we are obtaining!

Deep Relationships

Once you have come to know God a little through having regular times of prayer and through praying in daily life, you will probably want to deepen your relationship with him. And if you are trying to follow Christ, you will want to imitate the way he prayed and lived. One can imitate and adore him exteriorly as it were, rather as an object outside oneself. Probably quite a number of people throughout the ages have tried to imitate his exterior activities and behaviour, but have failed to imitate him interiorly and have not made him as it were the motive power of their living. Christ's close communion with his Father and his desire to know and do his will, made him one with his Father. This should be our way of life too, but it requires self-giving and great faith. It is easy for us to think that by trying to act like Christ in an exterior way we are doing all that is required of us. Perhaps it is useful to begin this way for our failure to imitate Christ can show us how difficult this is, and can indicate our need for his support and help. We have to learn to imitate Jesus' interior life of communion with God, for it is only so that we will be able to live exteriorly like him.

Some followers of Saint Bernard and Saint Francis in the middle ages were so captivated by the humanity of the man Jesus that they appear to have failed to see his divinity. Perhaps this happens with those today who are fascinated by Jesus only as a man. Probably the imitation of Christ in the West has been more concerned with the man Jesus than with the risen Christ who has given us his Spirit to help us and indwell us and lead us to the Father. But this relationship is difficult to understand until one experiences it a little and catches a glimmering of how God acts in us and with us. The Holy Spirit, if we let him, fosters our feeble efforts at living in touch with God and helps us to be open to him, for we can achieve very little without his aid, though we very often think we can. We cannot by our own efforts make ourselves God-centred. However most of us, in one way or another have to start with an exterior relationship, knowing about the outside of him as it were, but we must not stop there; we must let him into our hearts and let him touch the centre of our being.

As I have already said, if we want to get to know a person, we have to set about it in a variety of ways. We have to take the trouble to meet them regularly, we have to learn about them with our minds and our hearts, and we must give something of ourselves to them as well. We cannot expect to get to know a person well by only meeting them say, twice a year, nor are we going to get very far by just saying 'Good morning, lovely day' to someone we pass daily in the street. This may be a regular relationship, but it will only be superficial.

With God we have to have regular times for prayer and longer times, but they must not be just superficial. Also it is no use either simply getting to know about a person; relating only with the mind is not entirely satisfactory either if one wants to get to know a person. A marriage that was just on the intellectual level would be strange and probably not very lasting. Some Christian meditations seem to have remained on the intellectual level. Knowing about God is good and useful, but much of Western Christianity has tended to be over-intellectual. A relationship that is to grow and develop has to touch the whole of us. Prayer, reading the Scriptures, attending the worship of the church, and partaking in the sacraments (providing this is part of our Christian tradition) are all necessary if we are going to make our relationship with God interior. We meet Christ, the Word, in the Scriptures, in preaching and in the sacraments, particularly the Eucharist. He is their content as well as their inspirer. Our encounter with Christ will vary depending how responsive we are to him. And we must not remain just with the humanity of Christ, we must follow him risen and glorified, as he leads us in the Spirit to the transcendent God. How he leads us is not comprehensible to our reason, but it makes sense to love and faith. The way of love and faith and self-giving is mysterious.

Our love for God should make us want to do what he wants and to behave as Jesus did. We must grow in our desire to be righteous because the God we love is. We must come to want to live in the way we think God wants us to, that is to conform our wills to his. The prophets were always exhorting the Jews to live righteous lives because the Lord is righteous, and trying to show that the Lord loves his people in order to make them holy and not because they are holy already. And Jesus, in a similar way, exhorts us to be perfect as our Father in heaven is perfect and shows how deeply

God loves us. So we should desire to be perfect in our behaviour and actions because he who is perfect and who loves us, wishes us to be so. The perfection of God, the righteousness of God, may not be the aspect of him which touches and inspires you to want to come closer to him; it may be his holiness, his majesty, or his love, but whatever it is, and it may only touch you momentarily, it can make you dissatisfied with yourself. It can compel you to say to God, 'be merciful to me, a sinner', or you may fall on your knees and say to God, as the medieval did, 'you are all and I am nothing' or as Julian of Norwich wrote 'God of thy goodness give me, thyself'.

It is not easy to know or explain what it is that makes a person suddenly desire to have God as the centre of his life, the motive power of his living. The Spirit touches us in a way that inspires us to respond and open ourselves to him. We really want God and we realise that he wants us too. There somehow comes a stage when one begins to know God and not just about him. The words we have said and used in prayer, perhaps often without any deep thought, almost unheedingly, come to mean something more and with this can come a desire to give ourselves more fully to God. The need to lose one's self and the desire to do so take on a reality never previously thought possible. Without the intention of self-giving there can, probably, be no real deep growth in our love for God. The losing of one's life to find it in Christ is fundamental for the development of a fully Christian life.

For most people there comes a time, either through circumstances of life, or through getting to know more of God in prayer, when we have to decide whether we want our relationship with God to deepen and become more interior, and whether we are prepared to face up to the cost. This can occur in human relationships; we know if we go deeper in knowing a person there will be blood and tears, pain as well as joy, and we have to take a decision on it, and accept the risk of being changed by it. However, getting to know someone, growing to love them, can be either a gradual process or sometimes, we as it were, just click with someone and fall in love. It just happens, and it can be like this with God too.

Some people experience a dramatic turning, a sudden conversion rather like human falling in love; others are turned more slowly to God. The change in relationship occurs so gradually to some people that they hardly notice it, but they find they are letting him more and more into their lives and are giving more of themselves and that they really want to do his will. This sort of turning to God in love is a gentle conversion, but it is a conversion all the same. For others conversion can be more dramatic as it was with Saint Paul. They are clearly aware of a moment when they had to decide to give themselves to God, come to Christ, when they received the Spirit, or whatever terms they may use to describe it. However, though conversions may seem to be sudden they are frequently the result of a long, though often barely perceptible preparation. Saint Paul, for example, as he went about persecuting Christians must have been wondering about the power of Christ which gave them such faith. His hate for Jesus was probably very close to love, and when the vision of the risen and ascended Christ came to him, he was already in some way prepared for it.

People who have a conversion experience of the sudden variety often believe that people who come more gradually to know God are not really converted, but they must remember that not everyone by any means has a sudden conversion experience which hits them either in prayer or life. God calls people in many and varied ways and we must not judge others by our kind of experience! Evangelicals, both Catholic and Protestant, often ask practising Christians, 'Do you know Jesus, have you made him your personal Saviour?' Others nowadays ask baptised Christians 'Have you received the baptism of the Spirit?' or 'Have you let go?'. I think both groups want to know if we have experienced a dramatic conversion experience. But the Spirit can touch each of us very differently; no two people experience him in the same way. Love can be growing very slowly and hiddenly like the mustard seed; we can be relating to God in an almost hidden way in our prayer and life, if we have the intention of wanting this and if we are trying to be open in a relaxed way, accepting that God is with us and the Holy Spirit is already helping our prayer even though our hearts may seem to be asleep.

By being persistent in prayer, by keeping on at it, we can be led to conversion, and this, in turn, can change the way we pray for it leads to a deeper relationship with God. The aim of prayer is to make us love God more and let him more into our lives, and so prayer can bring us to a never ending series of conversions, to deeper and deeper turnings to God. If we have the intention of offering ourselves to God as completely as possible at a given time, he will respond in his own good time which may be instantly or slowly, in a manner that may seem far from good to us! His ways are mysterious and beyond our comprehension.

There are three points that need more consideration here; the first is self-offering; the second is intention; and the third is that God is more ready to give than we are to ask.

First self-offering; self-offering and being open to God can sound rather pleasantly heroic, but often once our generous impulse has cooled, we find to our horror how much is demanded of us. We have to give up our cherished ideas of ourselves, and the things we cling to for support and security. We find ourselves in an uncharted wilderness where we think we can easily get lost. It is dry and the going is hard, and God may not seem to be anywhere near, and we will want to go back on our generous impulse. Then we will have to persist in faith, and cry, in humility, to God   assistance. It is often in these times when we are reduced to helplessness that we come to learn more about the mercy of God and our dependence on him than when we are feeling brave and strong. He uses our very helplessness.

The second point, our intention, is very important. The will to give ourselves to God and be open to him is what counts in prayer and life. Sometimes our unruly affections and our natural self-centredness will make doing this hard, but if we have the intention, God accepts this however inadequate our efforts seem to us, and he makes use of what we offer. Sometimes we have to make do with only having the intention of having the intention! It is rarely easy for us to accept this, we tend to believe that it is simply wishful thinking.

When we seriously intend to offer ourselves to God in

adoration and self-giving, our way of praying will probably become simplified. This change may involve a need for some times of silence with God alone, if possible. Silences with God are always a good thing at any stage, because we are usually so busy talking to God that we do not give him a chance to touch us, or to reply in any way. At first, when our prayer is being simplified, we may perhaps, have pauses in which we are still and wordless between the prayers we say silently to ourselves. Or it may be better for some to say a short prayer or phrase, and let it soak in without saying anything, leaving the pause and the quietness to God, until as it were, the whole of our being is involved. Here we must remember my third point, namely that God is more ready to give than we to ask. The Spirit is there supporting and helping our inadequate efforts at self-giving and inarticulate prayer.

There are many aspects to this deepening prayer which can be looked at from so many angles that it is not easy to know how to combine them when describing them. We are each different and live in varying circumstances, and God is so great and so many-sided and can give himself to us in so many different ways, that it is difficult to do anything more than make suggestions about the ways he seems to communicate with us.

Look at the idea of being quiet with God in another way. If we accept that our relationship with God is deepening through prayer and our desire to get to know him better, we will find that as with other friendships, we start by talking a great deal and then go on to thinking about the person we are coming to know. This 'thinking about' in the case of God can be done by pondering on the Scriptures, looking at Jesus in the Gospels, or reading books about God. With people we know and love we reach a stage when it is good to be with them without conversation in a companionable, loving silence. So it is with God; in prayer it is good just to be with him and look at him as it were, being still and knowing that he is God. We must remember too that Elijah found God in the still small voice after the storm and earthquake, and to have experienced this he must have learnt how to listen.

Throughout the history of the church in the West there usually seems to have been people who prayed wordlessly and quietly, particularly when the life of the world was busy and tense. We hear about it in the fourteenth century war-stricken Europe, then again in the sixteenth century and at the beginning of the seventeenth century after the stresses of the Renaissance and Reformation, and, again today, it seems to be the prayer that the Holy Spirit gives to many. This being with God in silence, which was known as contemplation, was closely analysed in the latter middle ages, the progress to it was carefully plotted, and it came to be regarded as something only for the spiritually élite. Western Christendom has long had a tendency to think it could classify and tabulate the ways of the Holy Spirit! We generally seem to have learnt of simple, quiet, prayer in the past chiefly from the sort of people who wrote books and, who in the main, were intellectuals. Yet it is possible that many humbler people have prayed this way, as have the Quakers throughout the centuries, and, for example, there was the old man known to the Curé d'Ars who, when asked what he did while he sat at the back of the church, said 'I looks at him and he looks at me'.

The Holy Spirit appears to call a number of people to simple prayer today, and those in authority are, in the main, not setting about deterring them from it as so often happened in the later seventeenth, eighteenth and nineteenth centuries. It is no longer, fortunately, regarded as the prerogative of contemplative religious orders, nor is it seen as something that automatically leads to quietism and sterile inactivity. From the beginning of the eighteenth century until the beginning of the twentieth most religious authorities frowned on it and, perhaps as a result, many young people turn to Eastern religions in ignorance of the wonderful contemplative tradition of the West, which has been kept so closely hidden from them.

However, on the other hand, it is no use thinking quiet prayer is for all and trying to lead everyone into it though it may be the way for quite a number of people. This happened in some parts of the church with meditation of the so-called Ignatian type. Everyone was expected to use it whether it was right for them or not. I believe people in prayer schools today sometimes start off by trying to lead people into silence immediately. Some may be ready for it, but quite a number are left floundering if not drowning.

One of the troubles of books on prayer is that often they are written by people of great prayer experience themselves and who know God deeply and closely, but cannot remember their earlier steps and expect others to be where they are.

Everyone, who prays, however, must learn in some way or another to listen to God. In any human relationship we have to listen to the other, and as I have said when we know a person well, it is often good to be just silent with them from time to time. So with God it is good just to be with him in silence from time to time.

In the next chapter I will try and show how some people are brought to silent, wordless prayer, but not all will be led in this way.

Deeper Relationships

'Be still and know that I am God'. This, as I have suggested, is an important part of prayer. We should have a desire for God, want him and want to be with him, but at the same time we have to give up making efforts ourselves. We must accept the idea of 'God with us', and just be with him, in his presence without thinking about it. Somehow one stays with the deep imperceptible sense of the presence of God. He enfolds us and laps us round as water does a fish in a river or in the sea, or as the air does a bird in the sky. We are, in a certain sense, like the disciples who were with Jesus, though we do not have him physically present.

Some people find that this just being quietly with God, and the making of themselves open and available to him, which this way entails, grows out of their prayer and just happens. It appears to be the natural development of their love of God and faith in him. Others find that they are dumb and without words or beautiful thoughts before God, and though they know they want to pray, they do not know how.

For others it is not so easy to be still and know that he is God and they have, as it were, to work at learning from the Spirit how to be open to him and how to be still in the presence of God.

Others, God firmly puts into wordless, conceptless prayer. He holds them in stillness. There are, of course, other ways God uses to lead people into this kind of prayer, but I want chiefly to look at these three kinds of way.

Let us first consider those who apparently through an almost natural and spontaneous love seem just to grow into silent, conceptless prayer. Probably, however, rather like people in love who really care deeply for the beloved, it has not happened without effort, for they will have worked at their loving of God and made time for it. They will have learnt through experience, and through paying attention to God, what he likes and dislikes, and what he wants of them both in prayer and in life in a patient, open way. They will have come to live all their daily lives in close touch or communion with him. Like human lovers they will have given up things for him and he will have given them much in return. It will have been a way of dying and living, but because of their ever-increasing love for God, the giving up and adapting to his demands will not have seemed hard. This kind of growing into a deeper love of God that leads to stillness and silence in prayer which people of an affectionate nature can come to, is in the main joyful. It is a way of love and fulfilment in which the person concerned has his love purified by God's action, and his part is to co-operate with this action. The person comes to love God in an unpossessive way, not for the wonderful feelings and joys God gives, but simply because he knows God loves him and he, in returning this love, wants in all things to do God's will.

The change from a more emotional and conscious love

may be gradual and hardly perceptible, though in prayer the person will probably have stopped making prayers of aspiration and longing for God, because he will know he is with God in companionable closeness and love. He will have ceased acting himself and be content to be peacefully in stillness with God. Talking or thinking about the love of God would be unnecessary and would get in the way. He has then to learn to receive from God in a self-giving way, for 'contemplation is to receive'. All desires are satisfied because they have reached their objective, though the person has to learn to increase his capacity to receive from God. In this kind of prayer it is not easy to distinguish between our love and God's love, for God gives the love with which we love him.

Such a person may never know the pains and darkness so often associated with the coming to still, silent prayer of the contemplative type. This joyous, loving way of coming to live and pray in close wordless communion with God has sometimes been known by writers on the spiritual life as the way of affirmation and light. Personal and close love for Jesus both God and man, is often characteristic of this way. He seems to come closer to the soul than the soul is to itself, but yet he is far greater than the soul. The experience of God is both immanent and transcendent, and the two ways flow in and out of each other.

The people who find themselves unable to pray with words or thought as they used to, will have to learn to remain in stillness with God. The advice which I will give next for those who have seemingly to work at silent prayer, may be of help for them. Chiefly, they will have to realise that being dumb and wordless with God is prayer, even though distracting thoughts seem to pour into their minds.

Let us now look at the way followed by those who have, seemingly, to work at coming to this sort of prayer, which is often called active or acquired contemplation. It appears to us that we have to make all the running; the author of *The Cloud of Unknowing*, for example, calls it 'the work'. It is not always easy for us to see God's hand in it, though if he had not given us the desire and if he did not help us we would not keep at it, but we often fail to realise this at the time. The amount of effort which we seem to make ourselves, is one of the things that make it hard to beleive that God is helping.

What are the other things that make the coming to be still in the presence of God hard? A good part of it may be our concern for ourselves. We want God and we want to give ourselves to him, but there are a great many things in our lives, and our interest and concern can jump from one to another of these in a chaotic way. We have so many things to do and there are so many things to know that this is not surprising. These are not bad in themselves, but if they keep us from being centred on God, they can be. As I have already said, we dissipate our energies and rarely apply ourselves to anything for long. We have to learn to centre our lives on God and let him turn us (conversion) so that we view all life from a position that is centred on God, and so that we see all other things and persons in connection with or relation to him. It is a losing of our self-centred way of life to find a God-centred one; a dying to live more fully. We have to develop the will to want God more than anything else. This approach should affect all our living as well as our praying, and we should learn to accept all the disappointments and frustrations of daily life as opportunities for doing God's will and for the forgetting of our own (see p.132f).

In the first attempt at silent prayer, we will frequently have to put things from us that seem to come between us and God. The author of *The Cloud of Unknowing* says 'put a cloud of forgetting beneath thee and all creatures that ever be made . . . all should be hid under the cloud of forgetting' (*Cloud*, Chap.5). We must have nothing in our minds 'but only God' (*Cloud*, Chap.5) and not the gifts he gives us, nor beautiful thoughts about him.[1] Or to put it in another way, when we turn ourselves to God we have to turn the whole of us in as concentrated manner as is possible, only concerning ourselves with being with God. We have to learn to combine and concentrate all our faculties when we offer ourselves in stillness and quiet to God, and frequently when we come to prayer they are not at all united, or they want to act in their usual way. When we come to pray conceptlessly, just being with God, the imagination will want to act in its normal way, and the mind will want to continue to be discursive, but as we are trying to know God and not just about him, the discursive way will not be right, as he is so much greater than our minds. Making our minds and imaginations respond to acting in a different manner is bound to be difficult.

1. As the author of *The Cloud* says in *The Epistle of Privy Counsel* 'not clothed with any special thought of God in himself'.

This kind of prayer is full of paradoxes. We must just be with God, but yet we have a part to play which is not connected with minds and imagination. We have somehow to stretch to God with the 'naked intent' which somehow is part of loving, a kind of willed love; 'lift up the heart with humble love and mean God himself', and 'let nothing occupy your mind or will but only God.' *The Cloud* also says 'Do not give up but work away till you have this longing. You do not know what this means except that in your will you feel a simple steadfast intention reaching out towards God'; 'reconcile yourself to wait in this darkness as long as is necessary'. 'By darkness', he says 'I mean lack of knowing'.

At the beginning of this way we seem to be trying to do two things, firstly to offer ourselves in a kind of passive abandonment to God and secondly to be putting away thoughts and imaginations from us actively and stretching to God. We have to be both active and passive in prayer. In the *Epistle of Privy Counsel*, the author of *The Cloud* describes this double action. He stresses the naked intent stretching to God and the 'blind feeling of thine own being: as if thou saidst thus unto God, within thee meaning "That which I am, Lord I offer to thee" without any looking to any quality of thy being, but only Thou as Thou art, without any more.' God, however, gives us the love which makes us want to pray this way and he supports us in our efforts[2].

To expand a little, what is needed on our part is a firm setting of the will upon the Divine and we have to make a loving choice to do this. The will is involved and

2. 'Let God draw thy love up to that cloud; and strive through help of his grace to forget all other things.'

so is love which may be of an unemotional kind. This loving and vigorous determination is what *The Cloud* calls 'a naked intent stretching to God', Julian of Norwich calls it 'a seeking'; and Ruysbroeck says we must cleave to God. This naked intent, this blind determination, this cleaving to God, together with the realisation that we are assisted and supported by the Holy Spirit is, I believe, what distinguishes Christian contemplation from Eastern meditation. We have to cleave or stretch but we do not do this on our own; we need prompting from God that this is what he wants of us as well as the realisation that he alone can make this work possible for us. It is God who gives us the charity and will for the work though we may not realise it at the time. We need humility and love to start it. Humility or meekness[3] comes from self-knowledge; when we see ourselves as we are in relationship to God, we get a correct view, and are able to appreciate the self-giving love of God. As the medieval mystics keep saying we see him as All, and ourselves as nothing if seen apart from him. God gives us the love to love him with. Love, humility, and firm intention or will, are needed by each person who comes to the adventure of conceptless prayer. However we do not realise all this when we start off on this kind of prayer.

People who follow this second way of acquired contemplation usually have begun by talking to God and then have come to realise that prayer is a two way relationship between God and man, and that man has, from time to time, to be silent if this is to develop into a giving and taking relationship. They have, in one way

3. 'Meekness in itself is nought else, but a true knowing and feeling of man's self as he is'. *(Cloud, 13).*

or another, to train themselves to stay still receptively with God. One of the most usual ways of training oneself to remain there quietly, listeningly and attentive is by using short prayers. One says a short prayer, then is still and, as it were, holds oneself before God for as long or as short a time as is possible, gradually increasing the length of the silence. Let the meaning or import of the short prayer soak into you, or to use another metaphor let it flow through your mind without any forcing. Or say a short word such as 'Jesus', 'Lord', 'help'. You have to learn the phrase or word that is right for you at the time; and you may find this word continues with you throughout the rest of the day.

Dom Cuthbert Butler in his book on western spirituality writes of this kind of prayer in the following way:

'One sets oneself to pray, say for half an hour; empties the mind of all images, ideas, concepts — this is commonly done without much difficulty. (I think he makes it sound too easy.)

Fixes the soul in loving attention on God, without express or distinct ideas of Him, beyond the vague incomprehensible idea of His Godhead; makes no particular acts but a general actuation of love, without sensible devotion or emotional feelings; a sort of blind and dumb act of the will or of the soul itself. This lasts a few minutes, then fades away, and either a blank or distractions supervene: when recognised, the will again fixes the mind in loving attention for a time. The period of prayer is thus passed in such alternations, a few minutes each, the bouts of loving attention being, in favourable conditions, more prolonged than the bouts of distraction.'

John Edward Southall, a Quaker and Welsh scholar writing at the end of the nineteenth century tells of his attempts at this sort of prayer. A friend suggested that he should learn to be silent before God. He thought that it would be easy, but when he started, he records that 'a perfect pandemonium of voices reached my ears, a thousand clamouring notes from without and from within, until I could hear nothing but their noise and din. Never before did there seem to be so many things to be done, to be said, to be thought, and in every direction I was pushed and pulled and greeted with noisy acclamations of unspeakable unrest. It seemed necessary for me to listen to some of them, but God said 'be still and know that I am God'. And I listened and slowly learnt to obey and shut my ears to every sound. I found after a while that when the other voices ceased, or I ceased to hear them, there was a still small voice in the depth of my being that began to speak with an inexpressible tenderness, power and comfort'.

There can be many variations in this way of praying and our method of acting may vary considerably, but we have to learn to stay at it. This kind of prayer where we give up thinking and imagining can be very hard, particularly at the start.[4] Nothing appears to happen and it can seem dark and useless. It seems a waste of prayer time, but we must not shorten the length of time

---

4. 'For it be hard and strait at the beginning', *Cloud,* Chap. 26. It is very difficult to describe this prayer. It has no pattern and neither has any account one tries to give of it. Someone wrote of *The Cloud* that it ebbs and flows and has no shape. This chapter of mine I'm afraid is rather like this.

because of this. We must allot a fixed time and keep to it. Even if we want to leave, we must continue in faith, persist and stay there. You will discover ways that help you do this. The use of a short word or phrase either as something we repeat at the top of our minds to keep it (the mind) or the imagination occupied as it were, or as a kind of concentration of our intention for God. 'Lord', 'help', 'Jesus' can embody, as it were, our intention and desire rather than act as a mind-occupier.[5] The short word or phrase can be used in so many ways, for example, as a weapon against distractions, as a springboard for letting ourselves go into God, and, as I have just said, to embody our firm resolve for God.

Eastern meditation techniques and relaxing techniques may help, but you must not lose the desire for God however much you are physically relaxed. Even when the prayer becomes wordless and conceptless, it remains a personal relationship with a loving God. Always in the background of our prayer must be the cleaving, seeking or the naked intent. It is not easy to explain how this activity combines with letting God act and take over, yet it is something that Christian writers throughout the

5. 'Take a short word, preferably of one syllable . . . the shorter the word the better, being more like the meaning of the Spirit: a word like 'God' or 'love'. Choose one which you like or perhaps some other as it is of one syllable. And fix this word fast to your heart, so that it is always there come what may. It will be your shield and spear in peace and war alike. With this word you will hammer the cloud and the darkness above you. With this word you will suppress all thought under the cloud of forgetting.' *Cloud of Unknowing*, trans. C. Wolters, 1961, Chap.7.

ages have stressed as showing the difference between Christian contemplation and what they have described as false idleness, which would seem to be a kind of self indulgent relaxation, no doubt good for one physically, though not prayer.

With Christian contemplation comes humility as I have tried to say. Often by just keeping there we come to learn our own emptiness, hollowness or nothingness, and the sense of our own smallness and sinfulness makes us better able to cry for help to God with our whole being. Even if prayer time seems boring or empty, we can give the time to God in trust as a kind of gift or offering. By remaining we learn the humility that comes from self-knowledge, and God purifies us in this way, and in this kind of prayer God can penetrate to the very core of our being. We have to expose ourselves to him and let him get at us.

It cannot be stressed enough that persistence is essential in this second kind of contemplative prayer. We have to keep on keeping on. Sometimes there may be a sense of stretching to God, or at other times a sense of being supported by God. The intention for God, the seeking, the naked intent of *The Cloud*, may frequently get disturbed or broken, but when you realise this, you will have gently to return to it, perhaps asking the Lord for help by using a short prayer. Usually at some point or other, (and it is impossible to say at what point) people have to take a definite plunge into what seems to be a void of silence. This can seem frightening for we hate the idea of letting go. Here more than ever before we have to trust to God, not to ourselves.

I will try to give a few indications about the

characteristics of this kind of prayer. At the start, people tend to be conscious of putting away thoughts and imaginings which are at other times perfectly good, and are very aware of making great efforts themselves. We have to remind ourselves constantly when praying that the Spirit is working in us and is doing much more than we are aware of. He is both praying in us and revealing himself to us.

Gradually as one grows into this sort of prayer, distractions matter less and less as we come in some way more passive and less conscious of them. The prayer almost takes over and seems to happen in us. It is not idleness, though the self gets forgotten. The passivity in this prayer is the greatest activity a man can achieve. Here is another paradox of the spiritual life; complete passivity is the greatest activity. Somehow one cleaves to God and receives from him at the same time. It is not an emptiness though it may seem to be at the start, for God is giving himself to us in the silence though we may not perceive it nor understand how. God in some manner acts under, or above the distractions whichever way we like to describe his action. Experience confirms this, though we have to accept this in faith at the start.

When the prayer takes over, you are there with God and in God, and you are united to him though you may only realise this cloudily or dimly. The cloudiness of prayer contains everything and nothing. You may only know that God is, and that he is all. It is a kind of darkness where ordinary consciousness seems to give way to another kind of knowing. An awareness or kind of consciousness develops that is above other ways of thinking and knowing. There are various ways of describing this. You can say the mind or intellect acts in a non-discursive way, or you can say knowing and loving fuse, and somehow we know that we love God and he loves us but we cannot say how or why. The cloudiness of prayer has in it everything you could possibly desire. Words cannot express the fulness of it.

Sometimes the prayer has a flavour, ethos, a characteristic as it were. You may have a perception of being in God and with God and all this is connected with love. It can be the most wonderful thing one has ever experienced, but it is impossible to define how.[6] Sometimes one will have a sense of sin, either one's own sin or that of the world, or a combination of both.[7] In this deeper prayer one gets caught into a wider situation than one's own life and is more clearly involved with the whole body of Christ and humanity in general. For the prayer is a sacrifice, a self-offering undertaken in love and union with Christ for all mankind. Sometimes a deep desolation comes into the prayer, often connected with the desolation of the world, and sometimes an almost intolerable sense of being lost or alienated. Underlying the distress one may have what the great French, seventeenth century writer, Fenelon, called a 'bitter peace'. At other times prayer can be joyful and full of wonder, for it can contain everything and have a most wonderful fullness. *The Cloud* refers to 'an abundance of spiritual gladness', or it is simply good to

6. *Cloud,* Chap.26 '. . . he may, perhaps, send out a shaft of spiritual light, which pierces this cloud of unknowing . . . then will you feel your affection flame with the fire of his love, far more than I can possibly say now.'

7. cf. *Cloud,* Chap.40.

be there with God in silence. But none of these things can be possessed or held onto for as with any other kind of love, possessiveness kills. Somehow one knows without knowing how that God is working in one and our life changes. God works in you, both in and out of prayer, and you are more understanding|of|others besides coming not to want to sin anymore because of God. This is so partly because one grows in humility and partly because this prayer strengthens the will and helps one cope with the trials of life with firmness and wisdom. We may not think we are better people; in fact we may think we are worse because we come to see how far short we fall from the standard Christ demands but somehow one is more trusting and knows that God will support and help our weakness and that we need not fear or worry about this.

The change in our way of living is one of the few ways that we know that the prayer is authentic for not always does it have a flavour. It can be dull and boring, and you wonder if you are really praying and you may want to give up. It is however essential to keep on however bored or empty one is. In some dim way one may get a sense that all is well, but the sense can be very elusive! Faith is absolutely essential for this sort of prayer.

Deepest Relationships

I have suggested that some people just grow into silent contemplative prayer, others have seemingly to work at coming to it, whilst others again are held by God in deep prayer almost forcibly. The second group seem to need a kind of technique for keeping at it. However, the deeper the prayer, the more methodless it appears to become. Also, though I have indicated three possible approaches to simple prayer, there are many more; and it cannot be over-stressed that each person has his own approach to God, and this is why the classifying of states of prayer can be so unsatisfactory. Our relationship with God is an intimate personal one and, like all relationships has much variety, many surprises, and it develops with amazing freedom.

Nevertheless it is possible to learn from other people's experiences how God has worked in their lives and to find certain patterns of spiritual development. For this reason I want to consider contemplation, which seems to start with a holding by God and which can seem so surprising if a person knows nothing about it.

Do not stop reading and say 'this couldn't possibly happen to me'. Most of us tend to think that it is we who do most of the work in prayer because we are so conscious of our own efforts, but do we give God a chance or do we expect him to act in us? We must realise God does work, often almost imperceptibly, through our feeble, muddled and distracted efforts. A person who is taken, seemingly rather suddenly, into silent wordless prayer, has probably had the intention of offering himself or herself to God, often in a fumbling, halting, inarticulate way. The realisation of our littleness or nothingness before God can lead to a self-forgetfulness that allows God to work in us. Our protective barriers have to be lowered in some way or other to let him more fully into our lives. The sudden coming to wordless, silent prayer is often the development from something that has begun a long time previously, though like other kinds of conversion it seems to happen suddenly. This way of entry into contemplation is probably not as infrequent as may be thought, and can happen to very ordinary people, not only to the holy.

In this prayer the person praying can be more or less suddenly held by God, seemingly without thought, in silence. One appears powerless in the grip of God. The holding can continue for varying lengths of time, perhaps a quarter, a half, or even an hour. At the end of the time one may be so dazed that it is difficult to move about or to think clearly. Prayer may go on this way for a day, for weeks, even months or years.

During the period when the prayer is a holding, the person will perhaps find it hard to concentrate out of prayer on things not connected with God, and can appear to be very absent-minded, though life can seem to be wonderful and full of joy.

In the past there appear to have been two schools of thought about this kind of contemplation. The Carmelite school believed that it was only given by God to those who were reaching close union with God. They suggest this experience of passivity may occur very infrequently at first, but later on may become almost continuous.

Over against the Carmelite school there have always been writers, such as Cassian and Ruysbroeck, who regarded the suspension of words and thought, and the holding of the body in stillness, as a beginning of a closer relationship with God that can start fairly soon after a person seriously intends to give himself to God. St. Thomas Aquinas took the view that this holding by God, rapture, ecstasy, or whatever one likes to call it, occurs because of the weakness of the faculties which need time and practice to adapt to God's action on them. The Ruysbroeckian school of thought suggests that as we learn to respond to God and absorb what he teaches silently and hiddenly in this prayer, and come to know the power of his love, he withdraws the paralysis and we have to learn to continue in conceptless prayer without such obvious supernatural support.

If a person will allow, in this sort of prayer, the action of God envelops his whole being in a way not perceptible to the senses and reasoning powers, and a new manner of knowing develops which is above the ordinary ways of human description. All thought and feeling go, only a vague consciousness is left and it is, as it were, a losing of self without perceiving how, and yet is somehow right and is known to be of God and in God. One knows only that God is, and somehow self is lost in this knowledge. Yet again there is a sense of an inflowing of the power of God, and a seeming passivity of the soul. This seeming passivity is a kind of attending in stillness to the inflowing, or pressure of God. In this prayer sometimes even the dim sense of cleaving to God is lost, let go of, and one sinks into the abyss of God's being; or to regard it from another angle, God seems to have come into the soul and filled it with his presence. The vague consciousness of being in God is described by some in retrospect in connexion with the intellect, and by others in connexion with the will or love. Though this kind of union is known most deeply in prayer time, it continues, often uninterrupted, deep down throughout all the activities of the day. There is something about it that makes one love one's neighbour and makes one want to help others.

The effects of this kind of prayer appear to be similar to those reached in the more active kind of contemplation. The main difference is that the action of God within is more obvious, at least at first in the second sort, though the more active can become equally God-controlled in a similar elusive way. Anything can happen in prayer for the Spirit moves in most mysterious ways! The pattern is rarely the same for two people.

Some advice must be given about this sudden kind of contemplation.

Firstly, if it happens, it does not mean that you are holy already and above the rules of Christian conduct, and that you know better than other people on spiritual matters, though this will be a temptation. This kind of prayer was often condemned in the 14th, 16th and 17th centuries because people who had experienced it thought they were above the law, though the contrary is true. For if you respond to the leading of God, it demands the standard of living preached in the Sermon on the Mount, perfect interior obedience to God in love. If you let God take charge of you many humbling experiences will, no doubt, follow to show you how fragile you are, if God withdraws his support.

Secondly, when God withdraws the holding in prayer, you must not try to get it back by your own efforts, for this kind of prayer cannot be acquired. You accept whatever prayer God gives you. The mysterious things that can happen in prayer come from God and are not due to us.

Sometimes, you may find that you lose the way into the prayer. You will then feel lost and shut out, but you will have to stay in your lostness until God opens the door for you again. If you have not experienced this you will not know what I mean.

Prayer may become a blurred, dull muddle, and if it does you must just stay there in it. It is probably the kind of prayer God wants you to have at the time. You must not go back to reading prayers in books or such like. You must let what happens, happen. Remain before God cleaving to him, or just being with him as he leads, though you will not know that you are being led. The keeping there is what he wishes from you. Let him have charge and do not try to shape the form of the prayer yourself.

Later on after you have gone through the waiting in silence or darkness or whatever it has been, God may speak to you in the way he seems to have done with the prophets; or he may suddenly let you know in a blinding flash something he wants you to know or do. In the seeming darkness often comes great illumination. You may even see visions if you are the sort of person who thinks in, or is open to pictures. The ways God acts in this kind of prayer are numberless, particularly if you remain faithful (see Appendix).

Thirdly, various settings and trials can follow this kind of prayer both in life, and in the prayer. You have to learn to stay with God in the prayer as I have just said, and in life grow to be flexible and accept whatever happens with courage and trust. This is not a passive attitude; you have to be attentive to God and keep your eye on him as it were. It requires a certain discernment to discover what God wants of you and to learn how to respond to his leading in the trials and changes of your lives.

Fourthly, with this prayer, as with active contemplation, spiritual reading and attendance at Christian worship is essential.

Fifthly, when the being with God is wonderful and everything one could possibly desire, you will want to stay there for much longer than your allotted prayer time. Sometimes it will be right to remain. At other times when you have duties to perform, tasks in life you should do, people you should see or help, you must leave the prayer and get on with the things God has given you to do.

Sixthly, you will, probably gradually, come to realise that all your life is lived as it were with God, or in God. There are many ways of describing this, all almost meaningless, unless you have experienced it in one way or another.

Seventhly, often the person is given this prayer for a specific reason or for a task that God wants them to do.

When you have learnt to follow God's leading in the prayer after the 'holding' ceases, you may find that in prayer, God just is. You do not consciously stretch out, or go down into yourself to find him (which ever may have been your way in the past). You pray because, he is, and you are! It is so hard to put into words! You are light and free, free as air, and God is, and he always will be there as he will be there in the way he will be! The temptation to say 'look at me, I'm praying', is not there any more. You are 'one'd' with God.

Or to put it in another way, Christ ceases to be an object outside our life whom you admire, adore or imitate — he becomes the motive power or principle of your life. You are not only in contact with him, but you put on Christ Jesus and act in all things through the Lord Jesus Christ; your life becomes hid with Christ in God.

We do not know this through our ordinary powers of knowing, but by a certain God-given light we can suddenly perceive it in a flash. Sometimes we wonder if the union is as close as we think, and we panic and try to do something about it instead of being humbly and faithfully open in a passive way before God. Sometimes we just know that all life is lived in God and then it is quite wonderful. At other times when we are very busy, taken up with people and work, we doubt the union with God; then it can be right to say 'Lord give me peace and a sense of You', and it is good to try and leave the bustle even for two or three minutes to be quiet with God. You may not sense his presence in these brief times of turning to him, but when you go back to the bustle of life you will probably find a certain elusive calmness and peace.

The notion of conceptless prayer may seem high-flown, but there is no doubt that quite a number of people pray this way. I know them myself and my friends do too. You see many in silent prayer in city churches at lunch time.

This sort of prayer can make us realise our constant union with the Spirit who is always praying in us. Methods of prayer don't matter, it is coming to love God and live in his presence that is the really important thing. Christian contemplation is the experience of being loved by God and of living in this love.

You reach a state or way of living where you are that God may be. You do not know what you are like or what God is. God is the principle of your living and so close to you that you cannot see him. Since one just is, and God just is, it is impossible to describe. But you have a love and a courage that makes you want to work for God and for others; the work may be intercession for others or more active physical or mental work. This kind of love cannot lead to idleness or self indulgence.

Most of the great writers on prayer have stressed that when a person becomes closely united to God he cannot, as it were remain idle. Deep prayer makes it essential for the pray-er to want to go out in love to serve others. It gives the force or power which make it possible to serve others lovingly. I believe that this is the way our Lord lived and that his union with his Father gave him the power to serve and love men in the complete, full way he did. The great contemplative saints were noted for their energy in going out in love to serve others and this must be our way too. The deep love which God gives us cannot be selfishly enjoyed; it cannot be idle, but must lead to love and service in daily life. Loving God and loving the neighbour go closely together.

Problems of Stillness

In prayer of any depth, an individual is seeking a close relationship with God, but he may not appreciate at the start what this will involve. Various great spiritual writers have indicated how a person may set about entering this relationship but they can only give fumbling descriptions of their experience of him. Their inability to describe their experience is surely right if it is the transcendent, unimaginable Godhead whom they have encountered. Some have suggested that to find God and to love him with all our mind and heart, we need to unite our faculties and try to concentrate them in a blind stretching to God – a kind of going out towards God. They recognise various stages in this concentration when ultimately knowing and loving fuse. Other writers suggest that we leave all our senses and turn towards the ground of our being where at a deeper level of consciousness – the subliminal – we know God in a very different way from our usual ways.

But both types of writers indicate that this prayer can seem hard and that the senses tend to rebel at not being allowed to act as they usually do; the mind wants to act discursively or to reason; the imagination seeks for something to latch on to; the emotions want to expend themselves on various things and people. The writers also stress, and this sometimes gets forgotten, that the main agent in the turning within or uniting is God. As I have already said he inspires in us our attempts to find him and the more we are open to him the more he supports our efforts though his way of doing this may not be obvious to us. Writers through the ages quoting from the *Song of Songs* have stressed that when we pray deeply and silently, 'we sleep but our heart watches'. By this they meant that the faculties are stilled, but our heart, which they identified with the centre of our being, our will, or concentrated faculties, was in some way active in its desire for God and in its attention to him.

All this may sound complex, but it is an attempt to show that for centuries men have found silent prayer, being still before God, letting him act in their souls without seeing how, hard and difficult to understand with their minds. Nevertheless they have regarded it as worthwhile for in this prayer they come to know in one way or another that "God is", that God and the soul are united, and that this can be the most wonderful thing in the world. From time to time they knew light, joy, peace, love in a way as never before. They knew, as people know today, that the result of the hard slog is worthwhile and that it affects our lives and gives us a depth and peace in the difficulties, sufferings, and ordinary grind of daily living. Everything that is worthwhile in life requires an effort to obtain it, and the striving is invigorating and makes us grow. Often today people seem afraid of pain and of making efforts that cost time and energy.

Quiet prayer comes to people in many ways and not

all by any means have found it painful, or if they have, the pains have been quickly over, and like birth-pangs, soon forgotten. The way varies considerably for people's temperament and life patterns are so different, but it is possible to discover certain similarities in the way the prayer grows and develops.

As I have pointed out nowadays quite a number of people find that when they come to pray they remain dumbly before God without words, whilst some others are held still in silence by God. The people who find themselves dumb with God without words often feel distressed because they cannot believe this is prayer for they have not been taught about it. They need to be reassured that praying wordlessly and being mentally still or quiet with God is right and is what vocal prayer leads to in the ordinary course of events for most people.

The people who are held firmly in the presence of God know that someone or something supernatural, not themselves, is acting upon them. The experience is wonderful, and inspires faith in the Someone, whom most of the pray-ers seem to acknowledge as God. When holding by God is the characteristic feature of the prayer (see Chapter 8), the pray-er has something to remember and cling to when prayer becomes difficult, full of distraction or simply dead. However such a person may need reassurance that he or she has not done something wrong which has caused the holding kind of prayer to stop, that is if they are still wanting to love God and have not turned deliberately to sin. They will have to learn to keep working at prayer, and that being still before God requires persistence and great love.

The other group of people who come to a certain degree of silence or inner quiet in prayer seemingly by their own efforts, need to be reminded that the Spirit always prays with us and supports and helps our feeble efforts. We must let him teach us how to listen in silence.

Fénelon, the great seventeenth century French spiritual writer who suffered so much for his defence of quiet prayer, says 'We are always inspired. God never ceases to speak; but the noise of creatures without and our passions within deafens us and hinders us from hearing him. We must make every creature keep silence; we must ourselves be silent, that in this profound silence of the whole soul, we may hearken to that ineffable voice of the spouse. We must listen with an attentive ear, for it is a still small voice, which is not heard but by those who hear nothing else. O how seldom is it that the soul keeps itself silent enough to hear God speak! The smallest murmur of our vain desires, or of a self-attentive love attentive to self, confounds the words of the Divine Spirit. We perceive very well that he speaks but we know not what he says and we are often very glad not to guess it.'

It is interesting to note that even this passage seems to stress man's part in quiet prayer. It is no wonder that this sort came to be known as active or acquired contemplation!

Also it must be noted that God can speak to us in silence in a deep inexplicable way, though rarely in words. Also he does not always speak at the time of prayer. People get worried because they do not get an immediate come-back from God when they pray. However, if we are watchful and attentive, we will find that he does speak, but often later, perhaps through others, or again we sometimes act spontaneously in a manner that surprises us, and at other times we find we know something without ever having worked it out. By being quiet with God and letting him work in us in prayer, we somehow become responsive to his promptings there as well as in daily life. We tend to forget that our Lord tells us to watch as well as pray, and this watchfulness and attentiveness to him, to others, and to events should be part of our attitude in prayer. Learning to perceive and discern is very important.

Saint John of the Cross says that there are many ways in which God begins to disclose himself in the soul but all are secret, silent and very gentle. We could not bear his revelation if it was not gentle and adapted to our limited capacity, but because it is not loud and obvious, we can easily wonder if he is really communicating with us.

We must use all the means we can to assist us to be sensitive to God. The place we pray, for example, can help us a lot. It is best to keep to the same place, if this is possible. It is interesting to remember that Muslims when they travel take their prayer mats, their place of prayer, with them. It somehow helps to have a specific place which we associate with prayer, especially when we are beginners in quiet prayer. A church is often best if we can find a quiet one with a peaceful, prayerful atmosphere.

Also many beginners find praying in a dark place helps. Light somehow distracts. Though those who approach God through picture, icons, or a crucifix may find lighter places better for prayer. The main thing is to discover the place that encourages you to pray, and where you will not be constantly interrupted. We need all the external help we can get in prayer because we are human and very easily discouraged!

When we pray more or less wordlessly, it is usual to set aside a specific time for prayer. Quarter of an hour, half an hour, an hour may be the time we allocate, but whatever it is we should keep to it, and not shorten the time when the prayer is hard. Some suggest that we should stay longer when it is difficult as the prayer is probably more valuable than when it is easy. However not everyone shares this view. One thing is certain, the time should not be shortened because of distractions.

In every kind of prayer we are open to distraction, but nowhere is distraction so rife as in quiet prayer. When we go to pray our thoughts seem to stray constantly away to the things which we will have to do in the coming day (if we pray in the morning) or with what we have done (if we pray in the evening). Things which are of no importance seem to take on a new importance when we come to pray. It is hard to believe that just being there and letting the thoughts which distract flow over us in prayer, is what God wants us to do. But it is; experience has taught so many people that this is so. If one keeps there, not actively following the thoughts, but letting them flow over one, ultimately I believe, God breaks through and lets us know in some dim way that this is prayer. Often after waiting patiently for some time the distractions fade (this in some cases depends how long one has to spend on prayer time;

sometimes the distractions are becoming less clear when it is just time to end the prayer) and one can stay peacefully with God. If this does not seem to happen, the mind and imagination can be kept occupied by saying either a short prayer like 'Lord Jesus Christ have mercy on me a sinner', 'Lord, help', or simply by a single word: 'Jesus', 'Lord', 'Master'. But as Dom John Chapman says, these short prayers are not acts, they are a sop to the mind and emotions which hate not to be working in their normal way. The prayer goes on under or above (which ever way one prefers to describe it) these phrases though this is not easy to perceive or realise. It is God himself that we are contemplating, and as the *Cloud of Unknowing* says 'yet of God himself can no man think' – that is our minds are inadequate for so great a task. 'Therefore I will leave on one side everything I can think, and choose for my love the thing which I cannot think! Why? Because he may well be loved, but not thought. By love he can be caught and held, but by thinking never' (Chap.6).

There are various practices which may seem mechanical but which help in difficult times. The *Cloud of Unknowing* suggests that we cower under distractions and give up fighting them. He tells us 'cower under them as a caitiff coward overcome in battle' (Chap. 32) and this will lead us to feel our own helplessness. This does not mean we follow each distraction and the line of thought that it suggests, but rather that you say to God, 'help, here I am, I want to pray, not to be distracted; it is up to you', and then be quiet and leave it to him. We must not strive against the distractions ourselves for in contemplation self-action of this sort has to be given up, if we are to be closely united with God in prayer. And if you are praying as you go about your daily life you may somehow bring God into your occupations and life and so, in some way, the distractions about them are not so distressing because God is in them already.

People need frequent reassurance about distractions and the fact that God somehow acts in us under them. A great number of spiritual writers have said this, but I will only quote Fénelon who says: 'Distractions that are involuntary, these distract not love, for love is in the will, and the will has never any distractions without its own consent. As soon as we remark them we let them drop, and turn again ourselves towards God; thus while the outward senses of the spouse are asleep, her heart waketh; her love does not relax. A tender father does not always think distinctly of his son; a thousand objects draw away his imagination and his mind, but distractions never interrupt the paternal love; . . . such should be our own love for our heavenly father; a love that is simple, without diffidence, without disquiet'.

Almost worse, perhaps, is the sense of emptiness and futility or a kind of greyness that comes to some people, and makes them wonder if they are really praying, and makes them think they would be better employed in being active in one way or another. Not everyone suffers in this way, but the lack of any apparent action in quiet prayer can make people doubt whether it is valid and this consideration can bring with it a sense of futility. There are several ways of looking at this greyness, this emptiness; it can be, as has already been said, boring for the mind and emotions which at the start anyway are unused to acting in a way that they are unaccustomed to. Also as people, we like to know what we are doing and we like to think we are doing well, and this kind of prayer in no way feeds our vanity for it demands the loss of our selfish, self-concerned, self. This may make the prayer seem empty and pointless, but God also needs us to empty ourselves so that he can act in us.

It is also, perhaps, helpful for us when we suffer in this way to remember that as part of the body of Christ we share in the bearing of each other's burdens, of each other's problems, fears, etc. Emptiness, boredom, a sense of futility are felt by many today. Temptation nowadays is not so frequently to the lusty earthy sins which were such problems in the middle ages, but to indifference, 'couldn't care less' attitudes. Is it surprising that in prayer when we are trying to be open to God that he offers us the opportunity to bear with him the greyness and miserable emptiness of people today? It is far from pleasant and we would much rather have to bear something more colourful and romantic.

Again the dullness and emptiness can be God purifying us and his way of showing us what we are really like when all our busy-ness and activities are taken away from us. So often our activities are means we use to prevent us from seeing what we are really like for we are frightened by what we may see. We have to accept the emptiness, act simply passively, but, as it were, embracing it and saying 'Yes, I am like this, but you can make me different'; somehow stretch out to God whilst being seemingly passive. As I have said before we have to learn to be both passive and active in this prayer. We have to keep at it, and also learn also to receive from God. We are empty, dull, bored, for we are part of the modern world, but by accepting it and telling God to act in us we can be changed ourselves and change others. Because we are in the greyness we cannot see what God is doing but we must trust that somehow in the cotton-wool emptiness, or void or whatever it is, he is acting in one and through one. Faith, almost blind faith, is needed at this stage. What ever happens, try to persist in this prayer, uttering short prayers if they help to keep the mind and emotions occupied. Have spiritual reading to feed your minds and emotions out of prayer time, attend the sacraments, but above all trust God.

Fénelon writes of the kind of prayer that we have been considering: 'Never let dryness, or distaste, or weakness, make you give over prayer. When you are not sensible of receiving anything from God in prayer, then make a *prayer of patience,* and testify to God, that since you come to, pray, for no other reason but to please him, and not for your own satisfaction, you will remain there out of obedience to him ... we must be sure never to give over prayer upon account of dryness, but persevere in it constantly to testify our love for God. When God gives us consolation in prayer, he gives us marks of his love, but when we meet with dryness and desolation and continue in it notwithstanding, we give God proofs of our love and fidelity to him; in doing this you need not fear being idle and doing nothing. Is a servant idle when he waits in an ante-chamber for his master's orders? ...

'How can you be idle when you practise a great many virtues; as humility in believing yourself unworthy of any consolation; fidelity, the proof of which is to be given in times of trouble, not of consolation; patience in abiding by God, notwithstanding your uneasiness and pain; faith, in believing God sees and knows the preparation of the heart of the poor; hope in hoping against hope itself; charity because you give God the greatest proof of your love in that you seek His good pleasure not your own interest, etc.

'Secondly: a state of distress is very purifying; it destroys self-love; it conceals from us God's gifts to us, and what he works in us; and by this means hinders us from appropriating them to ourselves; it gives us a very low opinion of ourselves and of our works; and takes away a certain trust and reliance we are apt to have upon what we do ourselves.'

The great English spiritual writer, Lady Julian of Norwich says something similar. God tells her, 'Pray inwardly, even if you do not enjoy it. It does good, though you feel nothing, see nothing, even though you think you are doing nothing. For when you are dry, empty, sick or weak, at such time is your prayer most pleasing to me, though you find little enough to enjoy in it. This is true of all believing prayer'.[1]

Several famous spiritual writers have described the kind of prayer which we have been discussing as being in the dark (either of blindness or of a dark room), or as talking to someone who is not there; e.g. Saint Jane de Chantal quotes Saint Francis de Sales on this. Dom John Chapman says something similar about it: "I am in a dark room; saying words — which mean nothing — to someone who isn't there". He later adds "it is the

1. Lady Julian of Norwich, *Revelation of Divine Love*, p. 125, trans. by Clifton Wolters.)

prayer of stripping; in which all our natural powers are useless, all pleasure is renounced and we remain naked before God". Dom John Chapman continues to say that in the pure form of this silent prayer "there is no enjoyment — often continual worry — and yet somehow or other, it is satisfying, and *one wants nothing else"*. "The whole thing is perfectly inexplicable. But if it was explicable it couldn't be a contact with the Infinite!"[2] I think we forget in this age when we are seeing Christ in our neighbour (rightly) that he was, as well as being man, Infinite God transcendent beyond the grasp of finite man whom sin and self-centredness can make so blind.

I have been discussing the difficulties of quiet prayer because so many people get worried by them and need reassuring, but there is also as much that is unbelievably wonderful about it. Even in the middle of distractions of greyness which prayer can become, one suddenly gets a glimmering of light, or a quick knowing that all is well, or a warmth in the depth of one's being, or a kind of plucking at the heart-strings which makes one want to give everything to God and to do anything for him. All these sort of things can occur either for longer or shorter times, but more often, perhaps, when one has finished prayer time one knows a deep, and sometimes hardly definable peace. This comes to underly all our life and helps to make one patient in difficult situations, able to deal lovingly with the problems of others and even with oneself when one is trying and unbearable.

What I am attempting to say is that the continued

2. *Spiritual Letters*, 1954, 60-63 passim.

persisting of being before God, muddled, distracted, bored, ultimately if we are faithful affects our whole lives and really pays off. There is no other way of life. that is so rewarding or wonderful but for some people the prayer may not be easy. We must, however, remember that our Lord did not come to make life easy for us but rather he showed us the way of the cross, though resurrection inevitably follows sooner or later, and it is by dying that we truly live . . . So keep at it, take the plunge into the darkness of God, for some time or other, sooner or later, he will give you glimpses of light, and prayer will bring you to the knowledge and love of God which is our deepest need for he is the end of all our desire.

In the Wilderness

Conversion, the being turned more and more to God, as I have already said, needs to go on throughout our lives, but most people at some point of time are led by him into what I call a wilderness experience. At a certain point, or at certain points in our lives God indicates that we must go into the desert.

What do I mean by this? I think there are many ways it can happen. Each person is led into the one most suitable for them. For most people it means going away to be alone with God for a longer or shorter time, so that God can get at them without the aids and props we all use to hide behind.

The form that the desert or wilderness experience will take varies according to God's plan for us, and according to our natures. It can be an all night wrestling with God as it was with Jacob. At night we are very much alone, exposed and naked as we were at birth. It is hard to find a place to flee to when we encounter God in the darkness and in a deep-sided valley as Jacob did, but it is even more difficult to escape in the trackless desert. The length of time does not seem to matter; the desert testing can last a night or forty days. In it one is stripped of all pretences and of all possessions, and the possessions as I have said previously include past experiences of God which we would like to retain. Probably the wrestling with God is less fearful than just being with him alone, realising one's hollowness, poverty or whatever term one uses to describe our inadequacy. Somehow one has to be emptied and one has to hold out, and not run away. It is hard to explain. Somehow in the wilderness the soul is emptied by the silence of God and also filled by it too.

Silence and loneliness, and possibly darkness as well are part of it.

It is 'standing before God' as the prophets did. This 'standing before' requires our presence, listening, attentive, watchful. One experiences 'the silence of eternity interpreted by love' as John Greenleaf Whittier wrote in his hymn; 'Where Jesus knelt to share with thee, the silence of eternity interpreted by love.'

Silence, the timelessness of eternity, and love are three elements that can be discovered in the desert; faith is the quality which we need to have.

Silence in the desert has a number of aspects; there is the silence of God, the silence of the place, and our response to the silence.

God's silence has many facets. He can speak by silence; in silence he brooded over the water at the beginning of time. In his silence he can be very much present, but also in his silence, he can seem to be very much absent.

God's silence can be very frightening; the sense of his not-thereness can make us panic. But his silence can be very wonderful, communicative, and life-giving; 'the dark silence where all lovers lose themselves' (Ruysbroeck); it is the silence of eternity interpreted by love.

Love? Our love, God's love, the love the Holy Spirit gives us to love God with; the realisation that God loves us. The joy of knowing that we are loved. The silence that is luminous; the silence that comes from the otherness of God, from his holiness, his separateness, his transcendence. Without love it could be terrifying and one would fear for survival.

Holiness is the being of God in its intensity, and man cannot bear the fullness of it as he approaches it. Moses is told he cannot see the face of God and live. Holiness is aweful, disconcerting and fascinating, and it drives us to worship and cry out 'Thou only art holy'. The Holy is too dazzling to be looked on by man, and God is the one who blinds our eyesight. In the wilderness we experience something of the transcendence of God, who is so much greater and more mysterious than anything we can conceive with our minds or imagine. This experience can be deeply disturbing and wonderfully illuminating. It can be both pain and joy; invigorating and humiliating. It is an experience of the dazzling darkness that is wonderful above all else.

Can we find the silence of the desert in the modern world? You find it in the mountains. You can even discover it on the hills in the Isle of Man in the tourist season; utter silence, no planes, no cars, no sound of birds, perhaps a bleat of a sheep and nothing more. There is a feeling of union with all creation. God speaks in such stillness; you cannot say how, but it happens. Silence in a church in the midst of traffic noise can be the same, but this can be more lonely as you can feel in a strange way separated from humanity and creation.

Silence in a snow desert and in a sand desert are probably very different. Perhaps there is not the companionship of the hills. There is too perhaps, more fear of being lost and a sense of vastness which makes one feel small and insignificant.

What is our response to the silence of God and to the stillness of the desert? What is our silence?

God takes us into the desert for a purpose. Perhaps it is so that we may discover what he wants us to do for him, or it can be that he takes us there to purify us and to create in us inner harmony. As Ruysbroeck says, he can take us there so as to lead us to that single intention which aims only at God and to the seeing of all things in connection with him. God leads us to the desert so that we may learn to cleave to him with firm intention and love. Perhaps he has a special task for us and we need a wilderness experience to prepare us for it.

In the desert silence we discover our emptiness, hollowness and lack of true being *as well* as discovering the mystery of our self-hood. Silence is not just refraining from talking. In a way I prefer the word stillness rather than silence as our part in it. We do not like being still; we would rather be doing things, even going round in circles in the wilderness, or saying things just to make a noise. When we are active, we cover up our emptiness which can be frightening, and we feel in control and that we are important. If we are still we cannot escape from silence.

In the desert we cannot get away from ourselves as we are in our hollowness, and from God in his holiness. 'In silence people instinctively know that there will be nothing in the silence but the unbearable shouts of their frustrations, and the shattering disintegration of the false dreams they strive to maintain at all costs against the tide of reality.'

Silence must have a positive purpose. We have to be still (and attentive), and we have to look at God and listen. The Law says 'Hear, O Israel, the Lord, your God says' . . . It does not say speak, but hear, and God in the wilderness says, 'Listen'. We have to watch too; our Lord puts praying and watching in juxtaposition.

Pythagoras, the ancient Greek mathematician and philosopher, is supposed to have started the training of his pupils by making them be silent for five years so that they should learn to speak by silence alone! This is a bit drastic! The positive silence, however, is inner attention to reality, to the voice of God which includes attention to our own God-given nature, to the circumstances of our lives, to his voice in liturgy and Scripture and to the msyterious voice of our own hidden prayer inspired by the Holy Spirit in us.

We must desire to listen, to stand before the Lord, to be in stillness and we must want the Lord to do what he wills with us.

It is no use simply suppressing evil desires; a fruitful silence should awaken good ones. In the wilderness, God requires us to be still, attentive and responsive in faith and love. How he will deal with us there, he alone knows. We must never think that we will know what will happen next, for absolutely anything can, and we have to take what we are given.

The Prior of Taizé recently wrote 'God does not break what lies in man. Christ came, not to abolish but to fulfil. So as you listen in the silence of your heart, he transfigures the most disturbing in you. When you are wrapt round with what is incomprehensible, when the night grows more opaque, his love is fire . . . Then you have to fix your eyes on that lamp burning in the darkness . . .'

I think it is helpful to look at Elijah's experience of the desert for ours may follow a similar pattern.

Elijah often refers to God as 'the Lord, the God of Israel before whom I stand' (cf. 1 Kings 17.1), and I think this indicates that he served God by being attentive to him, or as we say today by being open to him. Like Balaam (Numbers 24, 3-4) he has to learn to hear the Word of God and to perceive what God wants him to see and have his eyes opened. Before his wilderness experience, though he was attentive to God, he had not learnt to distinguish God's 'still, small, voice' which can so easily be drowned, from the noises of the world.

First, Elijah leaves his servant behind before he goes out into the wilderness, for God requires solitude when he is going to purify us. Moses too, ascended into the mountain alone, leaving all other on the plain below. Jacob too in his mysterious encounter with the Lord is left alone (Gen. 32.24); his wives, children, baggage and flocks and herds had gone ahead. God, when he calls us into the wilderness somehow separates us from all others. Even if our wilderness experience is to be undergone in the bustle of the world, God somehow manages to separate us from our friends. When he does this, we find that the person we think could have helped us is in the north of Scotland, America or somewhere immediately inaccessible, so we just have to face up to God on our own with no support from others.

Elijah, just before he goes into the wilderness had had a great success for God in defeating the prophets of Baal. but the anger of the queen Jezabel forced him to flee for his life. His triumph had been short lived. And at the end of his first day in the wilderness, he was weary and discouraged so he asked God that he might die saying 'It is enough; now Lord, take away my life, for I am no better than my fathers' (1 Kings 19.4). How often we feel this, after we think we have done something for God, and we find others have not understood what we were at, and God does not seem pleased either. We can do wonderful things for God but they do not make us holy, and when God withdraws his obvious support, we realise our worthlessness. It is easy for a person to keep going when he is supported and led by God, and probably he will not have realised how his supposed successes have depended on the Other. Elijah had said 'I shall never be moved' but he now feels hopeless and tired. So feeling discouraged and helpless, he lay down and slept.

After Elijah had slept, God sent an angel to comfort and give him food and drink so that he would have strength for what lay before him. Though we may not realise it God does not let us be tested beyond what we can bear, but he refreshes us, though often in a hidden way. Elijah is then ready for his journey, but his testing and purifying is not over for it is to last forty days and nights. Some people do not have to hold out so long[1] but get there more quickly. However for most of us the wilderness experience is long and drawn out.

A person has to learn to hold out before God in faith and, perhaps, in darkness. Prayer of long duration is required of us. We may have to pray for several hours at a time. We can be purified by the sheer boredom of it. Also wild animals and devils lurk in the wilderness. It

1. 'Standing before' can mean holding out against resistance.

was there Jesus was confronted and tempted by the devil. The desert fathers, too, had great tussles with devils. For us, the devil is often the unruly part of our natures which resent the purifications of the desert. In the silence and emptiness of the desert, there come into our minds and hearts, ideas, emotions, thoughts and temptations which we never thought could occur to us. We cannot hide from them there for they come out and face us. It is a shattering experience not to be able to hide from ourselves what we are really like without the props and stays of our ordinary lives. We are faced by the devils and wild animals which we would like to avoid. This is part of our purification.

Also in the wilderness we do not know where we are going; we cannot perceive any clearly defined tracks. The desert is wayless, very dry and very samey, and there are no obvious landmarks for we have not been there before. We have to follow the leadings of God, and he seems to take us some very queer ways. More and more, we learn that his ways are not our ways, but, in the desert, trackless and waterless, and unsupported by anything or anybody except him, we learn his ways and we come to stillness and a listening and hearing silence. So it was that Elijah, after this purifying journey, was able to discern that God was not in the wind or the earthquake, but in the 'still small voice'. In the desert our ears get more attuned to God and the way he reveals himself to us in silence, so that we can discern that 'still small voice'. A person that has been purified by silence will not need words to reveal to him the hidden presence of God. He remains silent because what he experienced was too deep to put into words.

For some this knowing of 'God with us' is a still small voice, for others 'dazzling darkness', sudden dark knowing, 'silent music', the silence of eternity interpreted by love; how we try to describe the sense of God with us will depend on our natures and backgrounds. However, it is usually only describable in paradoxes.

After his experience, Elijah was told by God to 'return on your way', and this is very important. A wilderness, desert, experience sends us back to help others and to serve God as he wishes us to do in the world.

After a desert experience, I think we know somehow or other, that God loves us, but we realise too that his ways are very hard for us to understand, and we have to trust him more completely. We come to know that we must not rely on our possessions, and somehow we are more fulfilled and our faith is stronger. There is something purifying and joyous in possessing nothing; there is a certain lightness and freedom from clutter; somehow one is better able to say 'yes' to life as it comes.

Some people think that those who find prayer hard and a grind must be wrong, but sometime, somewhere, a person has to go through a desert purification. It is hard, but joy is mixed in it, and lightness and liberty. How it appears to us is probably a matter of temperament. Perhaps it is rather like strenuous physical exercise. A priest whom I met said prayer was rather like rowing. The race was hard, sheer hell, but rowing back to the boathouse after it was over was wonderful, and one never rowed better. Prayer time can be like this, a grind while we are at it, but when you go out into ordinary life, there is a sense that all is well, 'all manner of thing will be well', and you pray better in daily living. And life after a desert experience can be like this too.

I think something similar happens in close relationships, either in friendship or marriage. There comes a point when the relationship has to change. Probably some of the broken marriages today occur because people will not go through a dry desert experience, but if they had held out with the other in the desert, they would have entered into a deeper and more enduring relationship with their partner or friend.

After the desert experience, what then? This, I believe depends on how God has used us and taught us. If we have been given the gift of discerning the still small voice, we must follow God's leading in that. Checking with a spiritual director or guide is sensible, if you can find one and, one usually does, when it is right to do so. I think too, one knows when the advice given is wrong and this is often a useful way of checking the authenticity of our leading. Somehow God's own guidance becomes clearer if we are given wrong advice. But we ourselves must have the intention of really wanting to follow and do God's will in all things.

When does a desert experience come? It can come at any point in our lives. For our Lord, it came before he started on his public ministry and in it he learnt more plainly the nature of his mission from his Father. For Saint Paul, it happened after his sudden conversion; after his stay with Ananias he 'went away into Arabia'. For Elijah it was in the middle of his ministry. For the people of Israel, it came after their escape and deliverance from Egypt. I believe it happens according to the purpose and use God has for us, and according to our natures.

It can be a real wrestling with God where we have to come so close to him that we cannot see him, and he, when we think we have won leaves us with a wound and a new name and a change of character as happened with Jacob. We cannot anticipate what our desert will be like or when God will lead us there!

Interceding

In intercession we try specifically to bring other people into our relationship with God; to love and care for them in the light of his presence, and to draw them into the stream of love that flows from him and would draw all men to him.

Intercession, praying for others, unless prayed from a fully Christian context is not easy to understand. Yet this is the type of prayer that is most used by beginners and half-believers, and together with petition is often the cause of many giving up when their prayers are not answered in the way they want, or expect. Out of a Christian context this sort of prayer can degenerate into superstition. It is interesting that in the Lord's prayer there is no mention of personal intercession, though collective petitions are made. Yet Jesus tells us to ask and to keep on asking. For this reason I want to start talking about how intercession should be done ideally and then to consider ways we can start setting about it.

As I have tried to show in this book a Christian never prays alone; he always prays through Christ and as part of the Body of Christ. He should also pray with the full intention of loving God with all his heart and mind. This prayer requires a total openness and self-giving to God, and unity of intention. Prayer should touch the whole of our being and help us to increase our love for God. Out of this kind of prayer should come a love for our neighbour which longs for him to love God and be open to God's will in the same way as we are trying to do. Our relationship with God determines our relationship with man, though if we do not love our neighbour it will be difficult to love God. We can and ought to see God in our neighbour, but must remember that our neighbour is not God. Love of God and love of neighbour should be complementary otherwise our relationship with God and man can get unbalanced. Any spirituality which concentrates on man primarily, tends to go wrong and often becomes either self-centred or self-conscious. Every Christian in prayer should turn to God and offer the whole of himself including his relationships with others. This should be the kind of way we approach intercession, but it is not necessarily the way we do it, or even intend to do it.

All prayer should be a unity that includes in it adoration, self-giving, thanksgiving, petition, intercession and so on. However we are rarely united in our intentions, rarely single-minded, so when we begin praying seriously we usually have to tackle each of these aspects separately, but we must remember that ideally they form a whole. This unity of praying can, perhaps, be best realised in silent prayer where we can be more completely responsive to the Spirit and our prayer can come to contain everything in it.

We tend very easily to forget our unity with all other Christians who make up the Body of Christ, and often do not perceive that we are not praying alone. We must realise this and also we must remember that we share the same Spirit who is not only praying in us, or will pray in us and with us if we let him, but prays in other Christians and so provides us with a wonderful and deep unity. We are more inter-related than we would believe possible. Our prayers for each other and our attitudes to each other affect our whole community. By unloving behaviour, however, we can damage the bonds which link us. In prayer we offer ourselves to God, and through him we also offer ourselves to each other. In this prayer of self-offering we help each other. Close union with Christ should lead us to have closer unity with others because his love transforms us and makes us more capable of loving each other. Indeed, we should perceive our unity with all creation. The realisation of our closeness to each other in the Body of Christ is most necessary for intercession.

In loving our neighbour as ourselves, we should love them as part of the Body of Christ which is how we should regard ourselves. We are an organic whole and the pain or joy of any part affects the rest. Because of the unity of the whole body, any prayer we make must somehow include all our fellow Christians. Paul reveals the depth and the interior ties of this unity when he says, 'There is one body and one Spirit, just as you were called to the one hope that belongs to your call, one Lord, one faith, one baptism, one God and Father of us all, who is above all and through all, and in you all' (Eph. 4,4). The prayer of the person most given to God will be more involved with his fellow men because of his greater unity with God, and because of his awareness of the tie of the Spirit. God does more than we ask or believe possible through people who are in a right relation to him.

The most complete self-offering and self-giving was Christ's death on the Cross, and intercession must be seen in the light of this. Christ's self-offering of his life and death is most fully summed up in the Eucharist. Here by uniting ourselves with Christ's offerings we share in the most perfect form of intercession possible and in God's redemptive work for all creation, for it is only in conjunction with his sacrifice and his intercession for us that our intercessions have value. The author of the epistle to the Hebrews tells us, 'He ever liveth to make intercession for us'. Every Christian being in Christ and Christ in him is caught into the great work. Christ, as Lady Julian of Norwich says, is 'the ground of our beseeching', and the more we are open to the Spirit who lives in us and helps us to pray, the more we will grow like Christ. So we will develop the habit of mind and spirit which underlies the kind of intercession he makes for us and wants us to share.

We must realise that we are fellow-workers with Christ in the task of redeeming creation and to realise God works through us as members of the Body of Christ. We are the instruments he has to use to bring help to mankind.

Also we must come to see that Christian intercession is not a means we employ to persuade God to act in a situation which he has seemingly overlooked, or has to be summoned to deal with, but intercession should rather be an offering of ourselves to be used as part of God's purpose, and as channels through which his love can act. This something which we do alongside Christ.

How should we pray to God for others?

If we believe that nothing is more wonderful than loving Christ and living in touch with him, surely we must want that those we love and care about should come to do this too? Now if we have come to know and love Jesus, we will realise that this has meant turning away from our self-centred way of life to a more Christ-centred one, and that this is a costly and demanding process. This changing of ourselves is often hard and God's ways may frequently seem inexplicable, and only in retrospect does his shaping of us and our lives make sense. So despite the toughness of following Christ as the way, the best thing that we can ask God for others is that they may come to know him and that they may allow him to freely operate in their lives. This is the most wonderful thing in life; for it is true that 'our hearts are restless until they rest in him'. However this giving of self, as I have already said, can be costly, as can be the keeping on at it in prayer and life. But Jesus did not pray, when he left his disciples, that they should have an easy or secure life, or that all their difficulties would go. They certainly had not in his life! Rather he said to his Father 'I do not pray that thou should take them out of this world, but that thou should keep them from evil' (Jn. 17.15). This means, for example, keep them from despair, from taking the line of least resistance, from doing things from purely selfish motives, from the unbearable strain under which one denies all that one rightly believes of God and so on. Jesus also prayed that they be 'sanctified' or 'consecrated' in the truth and 'made one' as he was with the Father.

So in intercession, we should pray as Saint Paul did for the Colossians that they should 'stand perfect and complete in the will of God' (Col. 4, 12). We cannot know what God's will is for our friends, so it is best for us to commend them to his safe-keeping, whether they be in pain or health, and pray that they may know his will and be preserved from evil. However when we see people in great distress either physical or mental, we may feel bound to ask God to take them out of their suffering. Christ's prayer in Gethsemane gives some indication as to how we should approach this. He asks that the Father may take the cup from him, but he qualifies this by saying 'nevertheless not as I will, but as thou wilt'.

Possibly those who intercede are of two types, firstly those who are profoundly moved by the sufferings of others and are driven to ask him to remove them from the situation, and secondly those who dare not suggest to Almighty God what he should do, but ask that those prayed for should have the strength to do God's will and should grow nearer him *through their adversity*. Both these ways are good, but perhaps it is best to combine the two as our Lord did, first to say what we think the course should be, but then leave the whole situation in God's hands. Our Lord when he saw clearly what had to be done, did not wait for it to happen to him, but went out to meet it in the person of Judas. The principal thing that we should pray for is that we and our neighbours be preserved from evil so that God's will is not hindered. And when we ourselves know God's will we should go out and do it, and not wait for it in pious resignation.

The two aspects of intercession just mentioned, the asking for what we think is right and best, and the desire to do only God's will can somehow be combined. Our Lord told us that we should persist in prayer — take the case of the widow who kept pestering the unjust judge. So if we think something is right for another person, we can keep battering at God for this, having also at the same time the deep faith that whatever way God acts will be the right way. It is one of the paradoxes of prayer that these two approaches do not contradict each other. Also it is often right to keep on battering, all the while recognizing that God alone knows the right time for things to happen in another person's life. As I have already said we come to know people better by questioning them, asking them for things and for answers, and as J. Drury says we have to find out what God's will is by standing up to him and asking questions.[1]

We must remember, however, that much of our prayer for others concerns matters beyond our control. So when we intercede for others we must always trust that what God does will be right for them. We may ask that those in trouble or distress be taken out of their situation, but also, as I have suggested, we should combine this request with the desire that if this is not God's will, they will be given strength to live through it in a creative way. God's response may often seem strange to us at the time. We may pray that a friend should not go off the rails, yet it may be the only thing that will make him change his way of life. The prodigal son had to go away and get into trouble before he came to his senses and returned home to his father. We have to realise that we cannot understand God's overall economy; we only see a tiny bit and it is not easy to recognise how

1. John Drury, *Angels and Dirt,* London 1972.

this ties in with man's free will. However, even if our prayers for others may be short-sighted, God somehow uses the love we put into them. We need great faith when we intercede, and must trust him even when our requests seem to be set aside. We must never give up interceding however useless it may appear, for it is an essential part of our work as members of the body of Christ and as co-workers with Christ. And we must remember that the more we give ourselves to God and allow him to work in us, in our prayer and in our life, the more we will be drawn into the stream of intercession which Christ is constantly making for the world. By becoming more closely united to God we are better able to intercede. Saint James in his epistle says the 'prayer of a righteous man has great power in its effects'. We become holier by praying in a more self-giving way, and by doing acts of charity in daily life — for example by regularly visiting an old person we can become holier than we would by simply protesting about some far away evil. Remember Christ's own work covered a very limited field. By recognising our littleness and letting God act in us we allow the Holy Spirit more and more room to pray in us with groaning that cannot be uttered on behalf of all mankind.

For *whom* are we to pray? Obviously we shall want to pray for our friends and those whom we love. To do this may often be a pleasure. But our Lord also asks us to pray for those who 'despitefully use us'. On the Cross he prayed for forgiveness for those who crucified him. This means that we must forgive those that harm us for the injury they do us, and ask God to help them to repent and turn to him. We ask God in the Lord's prayer to forgive our injuries to him as we forgive those who injure us, which is a fearful thought. Our forgiveness can be so grudging and half-hearted, yet we expect far more from God for ourselves. Our intercession for those we believe have injured us must have something of the graciousness and completeness of God's forgiveness and so must our prayers for those who we think hurt us or, injure us. This kind of intercession will be more costly than praying for friends, for our forgiveness must be complete, humble and uncondescending and fully aware of our own need for forgiveness. We should also pray for the cruel and selfish people of this world, and for those who oppress others. Probably the evil-doer needs praying for more than those that he makes to suffer. We must not ignore such people in our prayer. We must remember that every evil-doer has to live with himself and this could be for him a very dreadful thing; we cannot tell. The cursing psalms burned with a very real desire for righteousness, and we would be better to pray for the unrighteous in this way rather than to ignore them as we so often do! We should pray with love and not self-righteously for the greedy, the cruel, and the unjust.

We also should, of course, pray for those who have any special need, e.g. the sick, the suffering, the poor, the lonely, those doing examinations, and so on. When we intercede for a friend who is ill in a certain way, we can pray for others who suffer in a similar way. We must also bear in mind that as members of the Body of Christ we have a wider responsibility for the distressed of the world. I think we do have this today. However we must accept the fact that we can't embrace the whole world in our prayer but God can.

When we pray for those in disasters or in war-torn lands, we usually cannot pray for them as individuals and it is difficult to know how to set about it in a meaningful way. We can, however, ask God to remove the evil from the situation, to help enemies come to understand each other so his love works through them and his will be done. As members of the body of Christ we must pray for the overthrow of evil in the world and in our lives. This kind of praying is very much needed in the world of today when the forces of evil seem so obviously at work.

The *way* we make intercession will probably vary with the kind of prayer which we use normally, but this is not invariably so. We have to find the method that suits us best. We must not be entirely taken up with the persons we pray for, but rather with God and his action with and for them. Some will make use of a rosary or say an 'Our Father' with special intentions for individuals or groups of people. Others may collect together the names of those to be prayed for. If this is done for most people it is best to keep the list short, otherwise we may become overwhelmed by names and lose sight of God. Sometimes this can be done by grouping people and, as it were, laying them before God in the kind of way King Hezekiah did with the difficult letter which he received from the Assyrians; he laid it before the Lord and committed it and his decision to his infinite mercy. We can do this with our intercessions and after presenting them, have a moment or two of silence, putting the people as it were into the loving silence of God.

Those who have a special need or who are particularly dear to us we may want to hold longer before God. This can be done by saying their names followed by a phrase such as 'Lord help them', and then keeping still with them and God in mind. As our prayer becomes more simple the pauses may lengthen.

We can also pray for specific people whilst we are performing daily tasks which do not take up all our mind (e.g. walking from one place to another, doing household tasks, gardening, repairing cars). The people with whom we come into contact in daily life will be more in our minds and probably more in our prayers than those we see rarely. If we see anyone in obvious distress such as someone blind, lame or sad, we can as we pass by ask God to help them. Each time we meet and talk to a person we should commend him to God. This will be more easily done if we are trying to keep ourselves turned towards God and some manner united with him throughout the day either by ejaculatory prayer or recollection at a deeper level. Many people find it helpful to turn into prayer what they read in the newspapers or see on the T.V. This can extend the range of our intercession considerably. We read about and see enough tragedies to keep us busy!

In the stage which intervenes between vocal and silent prayer, the ways of intercession will vary greatly. For some it is a period of illumination which God seems to work in their souls and make them love him passionately. Then it is possible for them to draw the people for whom they pray into their joyful experience of him so that they may share it in some way. If their prayers are made up of aspirations these can include short phrases embracing the people for whom they intercede.

Those who pray wordlessly will probably have a variety of ways of intercession. The whole prayer which is a giving of self to God for him to do as he wills with it, is of its very nature intercession. The prayer is joined with that of the Spirit which 'maketh intercession for us with groanings which cannot be uttered' (Rom. 8.26) and with that which Christ constantly offers for the Church and the world. We do not know how God is using the silence and darkness which make up the prayer. Before we start prayer we can gather together in a kind of collective glance, in a 'twinkling of an eye', all the people with whom we are concerned and for whom we wish to pray; or we may pray like Sybil, a character in Charles Williams' novel *The Greater Trumps,* who held the thought of the person she was praying for 'stable in the midst of the Omniscience'. This kind of holding a person in God in the midst of our prayer is a very good way of interceeding.

If we are particularly concerned with a person's problems we may find thoughts of them distracting prayer. Naturally the distractions themselves are not to be followed, but nevertheless this can be a way of intercession. Sometimes when a person has a special need it may be right to break the silence of the prayer and bring him before God vocally or mentally, but it is generally best to draw him into the silence where we unite with God. But he alone can indicate the right way.

Some people have the task of actively suffering for God. Some have to watch others suffer and learn to suffer with them, to be alongside them when they suffer. Saint John had to watch the crucifixion at the foot of the cross and see our Lord and his mother suffer

(I will touch on this again later). Later in life he was exiled to Patmos where, seemingly isolated, he heard of the persecutions of the Church. It is not to be doubted that he experienced pain and distress almost equal to that of the martyrs, and that he suffered with them in spirit. It is not surprising that he is the New Testament writer who is most concerned with love and who seems to know most about it. Ruysbroeck says 'compassion is a wound in the heart whence flows a common love to all mankind and which cannot be healed so long as any suffering lives in man'. For many of us prayer will be, as it was for Saint John, a being there whilst the world suffers, a compassionate yearning for it joined with Christ's. There is the double approach I have already mentioned. You have to put your whole heart and soul into being with someone in prayer and yet have complete confidence that God's will is what really matters. You pray earnestly for something or somebody and yet are at the same time deeply relaxed in your trust in God. We certainly have to share the loneliness of the lonely, and to allow the clamour and strife of the modern world into our prayer so that in sharing this distress we may lay it before God. As Michel Quoist's man, who prays in darkness, says:

> But, Lord, I am not alone
> I can no longer be alone.
> I am a crowd, Lord,
> For men live within me.
> I have met them,
> They have come in,
> They have settled down,
> They have worried me,

They have tormented me,
They have devoured me,
And I have allowed it, Lord,
That they might be nourished and refreshed.
I bring them to you, too, as I come before you.
I expose them to you in exposing myself to you.

> Here I am,
> Here they are,
> Before you, Lord.[1]

So it is that silent or contemplative prayer is for many connected with redemption or reparation which I will discuss at greater length in the next chapter. This kind of prayer seems to require a close union with God and with our fellow men who are united in the Body of Christ. If this is so it is not surprising if we become involved with Christ's sufferings for them.

Besides sharing the distress of others we can also experience joy in a similar way. Something of the joy and adoration of others who pray comes to us inexplicably and seemingly unbidden. Also our distress and our joy may be shared with others. We ought to have no pride or self-respect and should, as freely as we offer help to others, be prepared to accept it in return. Humility is essential for all those who intercede.

What I have said may sound very idealistic and high-flown. But such an approach is needed to counteract the very superficial, almost magical attitude which is often connected with intercession, namely that God has to be persuaded to act in the world, or that he is a power that

1. Michel Quoist, *Prayers and Life*, (Dublin, 1963).

can be manipulated. People tell God what to do as if he did not know the situation, without realising that he is always in it.

Two points must be again mentioned in conclusion. Firstly we don't know God's overall plan for the salvation of the individual we pray for, and secondly, we should remember that God generally intervenes in the world through us. God will not do on his own what he proposes to in conjunction with man. We are the channels of redemption and salvation which he uses, and the more open we are to him and the more responsive, the better instruments we are likely to be for intercession. We have to be closely involved with God to know something of his way and will, and we have to be open to our fellow men so that we can be used to help them by love, compassion, and by sharing their burdens. Intercession is not a superficial demanding for things for people, rather it is something which should involve the whole of us and at depth. Evelyn Underhill said 'Real intercession is not merely petition but a piece of work, involving costly self-giving to God for the work he wants done for souls'.

Sometimes we are completely helpless in a situation which is intractable and frustrating, and then our only prayer will be with the agony which Pascal says 'Christ will be in till the end of time'. Deep trusting faith is essential for intercession, and the belief that God cares for us and prays with us, as well as the knowledge that when we intercede we are drawn into the stream of love and desire which flows from God to all the world and which would draw all men to him.

Suffering and Reparation

This is another aspect of intercession and like the latter we can only understand it by considering Jesus Christ and here more particularly his crucifixion and resurrection. Until the death of Christ, suffering and pain presented an almost insoluble problem, though an element in the community of Israel had caught a glimpse of what suffering meant and could mean. The thought of this group finds expression in Isaiah in the chapters which refer to the suffering servant (particularly chapter 53). In these passages the sufferings of the servant, which were borne humbly and submissively, were regarded as being in some way or other a reparation for the sins of the nation. The servant may have been an individual, a person who had actually lived, or may have been seen to represent a group in Israel, namely the righteous 'remnant' which recognized that the sufferings imposed on the nation were for its ultimate good and purification. Some believe the suffering servant may have been the prophet Jeremiah who was driven by his Lord to preach a message of destruction to his own people. Jeremiah hated his message and often remonstrated with God about it, but he was made to go on, and was told that pulling down was needed before rebuilding could begin. Because of his message he was rejected by his own people and taken into exile in Egypt; his life was truly one of suffering. God afforded him little consolation, yet he obeyed.

It does not matter whether the prophet Isaiah was writing about an individual, or the righteous and understanding section of the nation; the Jews at the date when this part of the book of Isaiah was written found it hard to see the individual as separate from the community of the faithful. What matters is that the prophet saw value in suffering patiently and humbly borne and believed that he was wounded for our transgressions . . . and with his stripes we were healed, and that our Lord knew these prophecies and applied them to his own life and his mission of redemption. His mission was to do the will of the Father throughout his whole life, whatever the cost to himself; the Passion and Cross was the culmination of a life spent in obedience, 'He was brought like a lamb to the slaughter' (Is. 53, 7). Humanly his death was inexplicable and seemingly unnecessary; for example Christ could quietly have left Jerusalem and the whole crisis would have blown over; he could have incited a rebellion and achieved some success; he could have called on the power of the Father and routed his enemies by the forces of heaven. Yet he was only concerned to do the will of the Father, but the choice of doing it or not doing it was left open to him. He won the victory over sin and death, not by avoiding pain but by enduring its full force, and so breaking its power. No moment in his life seemed more useless and senseless to the world, and even to his followers, that when he let himself endure the suffering and death of the Cross, yet through him, suffering so inexplicable to the world was changed. Ever since the Resurrection his followers have glimpsed something of his secret and wished to share in it. Through Christ crucified they have learnt that the barren tree of pain can blossom and bear fruit for the healing of all mankind, and have accepted their call to share in the mystery, and this is the heart of the idea of reparation.[1]

I wish to discuss four interconnected points about prayer, suffering and reparation which can be learnt from the Passion and Cross of Christ.

Firstly the Cross was the outcome of a life of close communion with the Father and of obedience to his will. It was the result of being fully open to the action of God in all aspects of life, as well as being aware of the needs of man.

Secondly we, as individuals, have to take up our cross daily if we wish to follow him; we have to lose our life to find it. We, if we are to be Christians, must 'put on Christ' by endeavouring to resemble him and this means dying with him as well as rising with him. The choice whether we do this or not is ours.

Thirdly Christ's suffering on the Cross was really genuine human suffering, and if we share in this work of redemption we must accept real pain that affects the whole of us.

Fourthly we, the Christian community, are the Body of Christ. Christ has ascended to suffer no more, but he still lives on earth in his mystical Body, the Church. This

1. Reparation has two meanings: (i) the restoration of something damaged to its former state, and (ii) the making of amends for something which cannot be completely restored.

means that we have to share with our head in his redeeming work, however small and unimportant we seem to be, and, because it is done with him, it is in some way joyful and satisfying. Saint Paul makes clear what the suffering of reparation is when he wrote to the Colossians in the following way: 'I rejoice in my suffering for your sake, and fill up on my part what is lacking of the suffering of Christ in my flesh for the body's sake, which is the Church' (Col. 1, 24).

To return to the first point — Christ's life of obedience and communion with the Father: firstly I will discuss obedience in our day-to-day life. We have to imitate Christ in this respect as in all others. It is done by coming to obey God in all aspects of our daily life, and not only by following the laws which should govern our lives as Christians, but going beyond this by the grace and love of God and learning cheerfully to put up with all the petty trials and afflictions that occur, and to do our ordinary daily tasks as jobs sent by God to be done for him as his will. For most of us each day can bring not only joys, but trials, disappointments, pains of body and mind, the thwarting of our wills, minor disturbances of our comforts. The way we accept them makes all the difference to our lives; accepted as from God and as opportunities of doing his will, they can transform us and make us like Christ; if they are kicked against and resented, they can make us unhappy, self-pitying and self-centred people. The day-to-day trials of life can afford the best discipline there is, because we do not choose them for ourselves.

Self-imposed disciplines and mortifications are not nearly so effective and purifying, because we choose them — they are our will — and can often be a subject of pride. The discipline of the doing of everything as God's will, seeing his hand in all the happenings of our life, brings us closer to him and teaches us how to be responsible to his action and how to follow his Spirit. This is very important if we are to join ourselves with the bearing of the sufferings of the Christian community and the world; we have to be open to God's action in our lives as well as being sensitive to people and their needs. The accepting of daily trials as the will of God has a two-fold action: first it brings us nearer to God, and secondly in some way it acts as reparation. The trials borne as the will of God can be reparative because they afford the opportunity of turning apparently meaningless, trying things into a valuable way of serving others. If we can bear temptations, pains, the crossing of our wills and the like, as things sent us by God to be done as his will, and if we can unite the tiresomeness of them with Christ's sufferings, we can bear them for those who are afflicted in the same way, but who do not have the joy of knowing that they are joined with Christ's great redemptive work. Also we should remember that the training of oneself to follow the will of God in comparatively little things, which we do by the grace of God and with the help of the Spirit, enables us when greater trials come to be able to unite them with the suffering of our Lord in some way.

In daily life whilst we are learning to follow Christ's obedience to the Father's will, we also have to learn to imitate his openness to his fellow men if we wish to share in his redemptive work. We have to learn to be sensitive to other people and their problems, and come to realize they suffer the same kind of trials as we do; they also are insecure, lonely, often disheartened and longing to be loved. We have to be sympathetic to them and compassionate, that is suffer with them, and love them as we love ourselves — we get hurt so easily and feel sorry for ourselves, surely we can feel sorry for them in the same kind of way? And if they hurt us, we have to learn to forgive them as God forgives us. This sympathy for others, I think, becomes more possible when we learn to enter into closer communion with God in prayer. For the more deeply we pray, the more we come to know God and the more we come to know ourselves, our sins and our frailty, and so tend to be more sympathetic to others. It is closeness to God in prayer which I believe comes to make suffering valuable and give it sense. Also the closer to God we come, the more we desire to serve others and to bring them to know God.

The losing of self in prayer and communion with God is interconnected with my second major point which is that Christ tells us that we must take up our cross and follow him, and that we have to lose our life in order to find it. This is a crucial aspect of Christianity which is not sufficiently emphasized today, perhaps, because this is an age that is afraid of pain. However, following Christ necessitates a continuous dying to self. This death to the self is bound to be painful as we are so self-centred. But if we offer ourselves daily in prayer to Christ and at the Eucharist, the self-giving through the grace of Christ is not only possible but can be even joyous. One of the wonderful and strange things about Christian suffering is that it is often joyous. This is not strange really as Christ is not only crucified but is also risen and has sent us the Spirit both to pray and suffer with us. The joy in part comes from doing the will of him whom we love, because we know we are pleasing him.

In prayer, better than any other time, we can offer ourselves to God and let him penetrate into the depths of our being. We have in some way to allow God to take as much of us as we are able to hand over; we have to be emptied of self in order to be filled with him. This implies that in prayer, which should be self-giving and self-offering, we have in some way to allow God to act in us. This means, I think, that in a certain part of our prayer time, we have to act as little as possible ourselves. However, we are human and prone to distractions, so we will often have to use short phrases or short prayers to keep more superficial distractions at bay as I have already said. A short phrase, as Archbishop Anthony Bloom tells us, can be the embodiment of all our dissatisfaction with ourselves and a cry to God for help. He suggests that we should remain alone, silent — I would say before God though he does not. After ten minutes he suggests that we would be bored, after another ten minutes we would be so distressed at our emptiness that we would be in misery, and ultimately we would cry out with our whole empty being to God and ask for mercy — 'Lord have mercy' would then be a genuine and heartfelt prayer. Somehow by one means or another, by whatever way God shows to us, we have to come in prayer face to face with him, and ourselves as we are — that is empty, sinful, useless on our own. When we are really broken and useless with nothing of our own, God is able to use us more fully to help with reparation though this often seems surprising to us. Saint Paul frequently showed that the glory of God is most plainly seen in us when we are weakest. God seems to reduce us to helplessness, in prayer and in suffering in life, so that we may not hinder his power working through us. 'For always we who are alive are being handed over to death for Jesus' sake that the life of Jesus may be made manifest in our mortal flesh' (2 Cor. 4, 11). This helplessness and weakness can be very fully known in prayer.

We have to be broken by God in prayer in various ways throughout all our spiritual progress. This does not mean all prayer will be like this, very often our communion with God will be joyous and obviously full of love. But because God loves us, we have to be purified of our sins, and perfected and made more like his son. This he will do if we let him. In prayer if we can be still and open, we will afford him more scope for his action. We have to try to be very generous in our self-offerings. The process of our purification is bound to be painful as our shaping into the likeness of Christ will necessitate so much chiseling away of self, for God has to batter us in the same kind of way as a sculptor does to make a beautiful statue.

As I have already said much of this battering will take place in prayer when we tend to be more deeply attentive to God than at other times. It can happen in various ways; sometimes just allowing us to be there, being bored and distracted, is the way God uses. Sometimes God sends actual pain in prayer, it can take the form of complete emptiness, a sense of the loss of God, disbelief in God, or just simply deep, dark agony.

Unbelief can penetrate the prayer of even the most faithful. Well, this is as I have said part of God's purifying of us, but it is also something which is borne for the Body of Christ and for the world which knows these trials only too well. Somehow the two elements go together; the suffering in prayer as well as sickness and illness in life, can be something which both purifies us and makes us more like Christ, but also is something which is done as reparation for the whole world and the whole Body. We cannot wait until we are completely purified to begin helping our brothers with the bearing of their trials, for our perfection will not occur this side of death. So Christ uses our imperfect self-offering in conjunction with his perfect one for the reparation of the world.

The pain borne in prayer is real, deep suffering and not imagined suffering. This leads me to my third point about the Passion and Crucifixion of Jesus; it was real, ordinary human suffering. Christ on the Cross knew all the bewilderingness of pain which seems to occupy all our being and make us only concerned with enduring, and which does not allow us much apparent time for loving God. We also desperately want to escape from it, are ashamed of ourselves for wanting to do this. Christ was driven to cry 'My God, my God, why has Thou forsaken me?'. He was bearing not only extreme physical pain, but also had the sense of being deserted by his Father as well as by his human friends. Then he was bearing all the unbelief, the loneliness, the hatred, lack of love, desertedness, the fear, and mental pain of the world. We, as his followers, his Body, have to continue to bear in some part both the physical and mental suffering of the world, for the world. This suffering does not seem heroic and self-satisfying for usually, if it is genuine pain from which we long to escape, we feel we have borne it badly and are very humble about it. If we bear our physical pain as his will for us and let him bear it with us, it will not make the pain any less real and bewilderingly unsatisfactory, but it can be a sharing in his redemptive work, and in some strange way, a quality of joy will be added. In prayer we can share with Christ the loneliness, the insecurity, the boredom, emptiness and mental pain of the world today. This, too, is real suffering.

I think the bearing of physical pain becomes more meaningful if we have prayed deeply and become closely united in prayer with God, and realize that all our sufferings in prayer and life are united with the great sacrifice of Christ. Somehow, also through prayer, we can experience a deep unity with God which comes to underlie all our life and not only prayer. We may not consciously recognize this unity and God's closeness to us all the time, but there is almost always a dim, remote, realization of God's love for us and ours for him. We recognize that even in the greatest adversity whatever its nature, God is in it with us and that it is his will. Often the pain in prayer or in life may be so great that it does not seem possible that God should allow it or be with us in it. Or again we may experience unbelief in life in and out of prayer, and be horrified with ourselves at being unbelieving, but our lack of belief seems real, and God appears to do nothing about it and has left us alone.

Sometimes periods of pain and unbelief can extend over several days, perhaps a week, and this misery of them can be very great. Something keeps one at prayer, however horrific it may be. Rarely does human help relieve the burden if we look for it at such times. Of course it is 'I' who am unbelieving, but I do not want to be; this would seem to be a sharing of the unbelief of the world today. Possibly I am deceived, but the coming and going of the pain or unbelief is sudden; after it has gone, life in God goes on as normal. Sometimes in deep silent prayer distress or pain suddenly can descend on us for short or long periods, pain which has nothing to do with physical weakness. This I believe is a sharing of the suffering of the world. Like physical pain it comes to us; it is not sought but is something God gives us to bear. Like extreme physical pain, we have no sense of being able to do more than survive, but because we have prayed deeply and are united to God and because God is always in the heart of it though we don't see him, it is valuable for us and for the world. Saint Catherine of Siena knew this sort of thing. Once after having been severely tempted to sin in a way that was loathsome to her, she asked God where he had been whilst she was enduring such torments, and he told her that he was in the midst of it with her helping though she did not see him. This endurance would be impossible without his being in it with us. There is nothing passive in our endurance for it is by a sheer effort of will that we cling to the God who does not seem to be there. A crucifix can be a great help at such times.

The pain and suffering which I have been describing is not chosen voluntarily — we are given no option about having it, though we can choose the way we accept it. There is, however, another kind of suffering which we may have a choice about. It is the kind which our Lord's mother and Saint John knew at the foot of the Cross; they did not need to be there, but could have hidden themselves away from it and refused to share in it. But because their love for Jesus was so great they wanted to be there and by their presence share his suffering. Our Lord's mother, who had no sin of her own to atone for, had her soul pierced, as it were, by a sword and was drawn in some way into sharing her son's work of reparation. Throughout the centuries those who have been closest to Christ seem to have shared most closely the fellowship of his suffering.

This links with my fourth point which I made at the beginning of this chapter. We have a unity of love with each other because of our unity with our suffering Lord; as the Body of Christ we all share each other's burdens. Christ bore the greatest burden of mankind, namely sin with all its attendant suffering on the Cross, and there is a real sense in which we, his mystical Body on earth, in some way continue bearing it. It is important that as members of the body we recognize this and fulfil this task in union with him. There is a delicate and spiritual relationship between the members of the body of Christ, and as Saint Paul has said all its members suffer with each other (1 Cor. 12, 26). Because of this unity we can in some way share in the sufferings of those who like our Lord are actively suffering on the Cross though we may not be actually on it ourselves. The distress of Mary was very real and her sharing of the sufferings of her son was no illusion, because of her very great love for him. For some people their sharing in the work of reparation consists in having deep compassion with those who suffer, because they themselves are united and given to Christ, and because they see Christ suffering in others. This kind of reparation like all others should be based on self-giving to God, which should lead us to love our fellow men. We have to be open to God, and open to men. Through Christ we can in our prayer agonize for others, as Saint Paul urges the Christians in Rome to strive together in their prayers for him, using a word meaning 'to agonize with' him. This agonizing for each other can be done practically in our help and care for the sick, the lonely, the mentally distressed, but it can be done too in prayer if we are exposing ourselves to the love of God.

It often works in what may seem strange ways, which the unbelieving might consider self-delusory. If a friend is in some kind of agony, mental or physical, in prayer time or out of prayer time, we may be called to suffer with him. Their fears somehow consume us, sometimes for quite long periods or for short times. I think it is something deeper than simple human sympathy. If the period of suffering with the person is short it may be extremely intensive and physically exhausting. Sometimes this kind of pain comes suddenly and it has simply to be accepted and borne in some way in connection with the sufferings of Christ. Other times we are given an option either to accept or reject the bearing of it. This is a small and hidden way of suffering for the world.

There are a variety of ways in which we can suffer with each other. In some of the ways we will not at the time at least be conscious that we are suffering for others, and in other ways we will have to make a deliberate effort to suffer with or for specific people. I think any suffering for others has for a Christian to be linked with the sufferings of Christ. Suffering with Christ for the world has always been part of the Franciscan tradition. Saint Bonaventure, the first theologian of the Franciscan order and a devoted follower of Saint Francis, saw the Cross as the resting place of the soul before its closest union with God. The stigmata of Saint Francis were seen as external evidence of his close union with Christ. Bonaventure believed that if we were united to Christ we would be willing to die for our neighbour's salvation. Love of neighbour was so closely connected with love of God. Benet of Canfield, a sixteenth-century Franciscan, also a devoted follower of Saint Francis, thought that in the highest contemplation our sufferings could not be seen except as those of Christ. Christ so lived in him that he could say with Saint Paul that he was crucified with Christ, 'nevertheless not he, but Christ lived in him'. If our sufferings and Christ's are contemplated as one and the same, it follows that we share in some degree the sufferings of the other members of the Body of Christ. Devotion to Christ in some way carries with it suffering for the brethren particularly at times of closest union when we are most closely united to him. This helps explain the darkness of pain and the utter emptiness and sense of complete futility that can come in wordless prayer. As many people today have a fear of emptiness, it is not surprising if we who are the Body of Christ share this. Boredom, inexplicable unbelief, a sense of insecurity and futility also occur in more conscious forms of prayer and these also are symptoms of the malaise of the world which we have to share. The closer the union, the deeper and less understandable will be the pain. Also we will not always know that we are enduring it for others such is the nature of darkness. This I would think was the case with Padre Pio; surely in bearing the wounds and pains of the Christ in his body, he was sharing in the redemptive suffering for the world in a way that was understandable to the people around about him. He was afraid of dying, because he knew what graces and gifts God had given him and how little he had made of them. This was, perhaps, only part of the truth; in knowing this fear he was sharing in the fear of death that so many people have today. His fear had to be real to make it genuine sharing. In the opera *The Carmelites* the mother superior, a woman of great holiness, dies extremely badly. At the end of the opera when a cowardly nun dies bravely on the guillotine during the French revolution, we come to realize that the mother superior had taken upon her the fear of death which this nun had. This is a dramatization of an experience which a number of devout Christians have though they may not always recognize why they are suffering in such ways, let alone for whom they are suffering.

Sometimes we can choose to suffer for other people in a more deliberate way. Something is seen of this in 2 Corinthians, chapter 11, where Saint Paul tells us that besides bearing his own burdens, he shares other people's, 'Who is sick at heart and I am not sick, who falls from grace and I do not die of shame'. Austin Farrer writes of this passage, 'Saint Paul takes his friends to his heart, both for good and for ill. It is the living out of our unity in Christ that we should care for one another with the heart of Christ, and by our prayers throw ourselves into the deepest concerns of our friends. Let us not offer the

Eucharist without praying for some other man as though we were that man himself. It is an excellent thing indeed, often to say all the prayers of the Eucharist in the place and in the person of another man saying them; being that man in God's sight as far as we know how.'[2] Saint Catherine of Siena did this kind of thing but in a very wholehearted way. Appalled by the schism and disunity of the church and by the corruption of the clergy, she offered her life to God for the reparation of these sins, and in prayer she suffered for people to the point of extreme exhaustion. She linked her sufferings with the blood of Christ. Later people were to associate such sufferings with the heart of Jesus. The deliberate self-offering of one's whole being to God for specific evils is not a way which many will be called to follow, but it is a valuable and possible one.

We have, however, to learn from God what is the way he wishes us to follow, but in one way or another we must share in the work of reparation, for this privilege must belong to every member of the mystical Body of Christ. We have to remember that this work must always be undertaken in a spirit of simplicity and humility, and must always be linked with Our Lord's offering of himself on the Cross. Though we must be crucified with Christ, the amount of suffering is not the important thing, the essential thing is perfect obedience to the Father's will. Our Lord summed up his work of reparation in the following words, 'For their sakes I sanctify myself that they may also be sanctified in truth' (John 17, 19). We are, as his followers, included in the self-dedication of Jesus. It necessitates the glad giving

2. *The Crown of the Year*, London 1954, p. 20.

of the whole of ourselves in purity and love to God to be united with him in his work of redemption. This embraces the whole of life, its joyousness as well as its painful aspects.

Our reparation can only be a token of our love, for Our Lord made 'one full perfect and sufficient sacrifice and oblation and satisfaction for the sins of the world'. However by being united more closely to him in his perfect work, we can learn more clearly the meaning of suffering and how to use it rightly, and how joyous this can be for we suffer it with him for others as others do for us.

Shared Prayer

Christians come together to pray in groups in many parts of Britain today besides worshipping in church on Sundays. Groups can be denominational but quite often they are interdenominational, and these meetings are amongst the most fruitful ecumenical activities that exist just now. This praying together is often known as shared prayer, and this is a good name for it, since we come to share together in our praising, adoring and worshipping and petitioning of God. As our Lord told us that he would be there when two or three gathered together in his name, surely it is right that we should pray in this way? Also it helps us to realise more deeply the bonds which link us together as christians.

It is not easy to lay down schemes for this kind of prayer, any more than it is to try to instruct in prayer an individual whom one does not know well. As each individual has his own relationship with God and his own way of prayer to which God leads him, so has each prayer-group. It is possible, however, to give a few guide-lines.

First we have to remember that Catholics and Protestants have been praying in groups for centuries. Family-prayers were a feature of daily life amongst all denominations until comparatively recently, and

Evangelical prayer-meetings have been going on for many years. So this kind of praying is nothing new.

The prayer of the group should be truly shared, and the prayer should be something that everyone tries to pray together. When someone prays in a way we do not understand, we should ask the Spirit to give us under-standing. So it is helpful before we start in a group to say privately a prayer like, 'Help me to enter into the prayer of others,' and ask God to give us the grace not to be critical of their forms of expression or theology.

To prevent one person monopolising the session, it can be suggested to the group that each should try to keep their vocal prayers short. However, concern for brevity must not take away individual liberty and openness to the Spirit. One should aim at praying to the point, and not saying anything unnecessary, and not saying something just to break a silence which might develop into something very fruitful for the group. We must above all follow the leading of the Spirit, and not our own natural inclination.

It is probably best for groups to change their leader at each session, but again experience alone will show what is right in each particular situation. However such a course may prevent one individual continually dominating.

Secondly, it must be realised that shared prayer can have many facets, forms and ways. It can be vocal or silent, or there can be singing, or it can be a combination of all these. Some people are put off because they either fear they may be expected to talk in tongues at such a group or that others will, and this might be embarrassing. For a number of reasons people can be very shy of praying with others. The Holy Spirit moves in many ways, and he may equally lead to a deep shared silence which is one of the most wonderful ways of praying. I believe that the kind of shared prayer where vocal prayer is combined with shared silence can be very worthwhile. Besides breaking down barriers between individuals and making our awareness of the action of the Spirit deeper, it encourages those who pray vocally to learn the value of silent prayer, and can help lead them to more attentive listening to God in their personal prayer.

Thirdly, the size of the group and its composition are important. The location and length of time spent on the prayer also need consideration. Six or seven people are probably the best number for a group but up to ten is workable, though if people have a common aim a larger group is possible. An ecumenical collection of people affords opportunities of learning from each other about different traditions of prayer; somehow by praying with people of another tradition one widens one's own knowledge of God and of prayer.

Probably each group needs to have at least two people who pray regularly and deeply in order to give an anchor or roots to the meeting. People who are neurotic or in some way disturbed can easily upset the group unless there is a firm core of regularly praying Christians. In groups without such a core, if things go wrong, the forces of evil may gain a foothold and the results could be very disturbing. I do not think we are sufficiently aware of this sort of danger.

Fourthly, and of great importance, we come together united in Christ and supported by the Spirit primarily to praise and adore God and, only secondly, to make intercessions and petitions for others and ourselves. In this we must follow the pattern of the Lord's prayer. Praise and adoration unite us before we name our own requests.

Fifthly, and also extremely important, is the fact that shared prayer should not take the place of our own personal daily prayer, but should rather deepen it. The two ways of prayer should strengthen each other, and help us to grow in faith and love of God and of the other members of the body of Christ. As I have said, we never pray alone even when we are on our own, but always as members of the Body of Christ, the Church. By praying together under the guidance of the Holy Spirit, we can come to a deeper realisation of the communion of saints to which we belong, and of the wonderful inter-relatedness of all humanity, and, indeed, of all creation.

Shared prayer can be an enormous help to us when we go through times of dryness and darkness in personal prayer or when we are in difficulty or sorrow. Also today there are some people who find starting to pray on their own very difficult, whereas praying in a group comes more easily to them, and once they can enter into a relationship with God in the group, they can continue on their own. Members of a group who pray regularly can be of great assistance to such beginners. However, for most people shared prayer should encourage them to go deeper in personal prayer, though we must always remember that God's gift of prayer is not just for us as individuals but for the sake of the whole Body of Christ.

Sixthly, it is good for a group to have a common

theme or topic. Many groups begin by studying a portion of Scripture together or by having a section from the Bible read aloud, or some find it helpful to have read on their own such a portion prior to the meeting and then discuss it before prayer. This helps us to start with God and have our attention fixed on him rather than ourselves or the people we are praying for.

There are many other aspects of shared prayer that could be touched on. It is certainly enormously worthwhile and can help us to grow in love of God and of each other as fellow members of the Body of Christ, and to increase our sense of fellowship, after all we should have a profound fellowship because we share a common life in Christ. As in all prayer, it needs great openness on our part, and honesty, to be ourselves with God and each other; for we cannot pretend to be other than we are, and it demands great charity and understanding of ourselves and others. It can be very demanding and very liberating and can bring great peace. It is in fact very worthwhile.

Conclusion

How do you get to know a person, and how do you know that you know a person? I have tried to show how I think we can relate to God, and I would like now to try to sum up a little.

I suggest that you get to know someone through meeting frequently, through being with them in conversation and conversation includes listening as well as talking, through learning about them with your mind, through argument, through being open and giving something of yourself, through letting friendship develop freely and spontaneously, and through being with them in deep, companionable silence. Knowing covers all this and more. It is not easy to put into words all that deep friendship includes. It is something which we experience, and dissecting it or finding terms to describe the wonder of it is difficult. Also our relationships never stay quite the same, and we never know anyone completely, which is not surprising as we never fully understand ourselves.

Relating to God in depth is far more wonderful and far harder to describe because of the mysterious nature of God, who is transcendent, all-holy and unknowable but who is also immanent and close. When we love someone deeply, we can forget ourselves in the wonder of the other, and in our desire to please them. This can happen to us if we become so captivated by God that he becomes the All of our lives, and we look at him rather than ourselves. We forget ourselves and what we want in our concern to do what he wants. We become pure in heart and poor in spirit; that is we do not want anything for ourselves, but only God and all things for God. This is something that we can only come to know by experience, if we let go of ourselves and accept that God loves us, and let him live in us and through us. Remember he is the living God whom we can know by a living experience. One of the first requirements, if we want to relate to God, is to believe that he takes the initiative. He loves us even before we realise that we are capable of loving and he gives us his Spirit to help us pray and relate to him.

Let us look more closely at what we must do in order to develop a relationship with God, and when we do this we must remember that because we are all different, no two persons will relate in quite the same way. Also, though I number the following aspects of relating and experiencing God, they do not necessarily happen in this order, but are often concurrent. They are all part of getting to know God and inter-relate with each other.

Firstly, meeting frequently and regularly is important. I have tried to make this clear though I know only too well that it is not possible for some people to have the same time for prayer each day, or even times of the same length, or in the same place. But the ideal is to have fixed, regular times each day, in the same place, especially if you are a beginner. For those who have come to deep silent prayer, greater flexibility is possible and permissible. It is also important to remember in some way or another to turn to God in prayer in daily life, because we must learn to live all our lives in touch with God, and so be open to his promptings. Life and prayer interact closely on each other if we live in this way, and there is no difference between the sacred and secular for we will live all our life in the presence of God.

Secondly, look at conversation with God. In conversation with God, we tell him about ourselves, our needs, our joys, the needs of our friends, our sins, and everything that happens we share with him in the same kind of way that the disciples shared their lives with Jesus. He also shared his life with them, but often they did not understand what he was trying to tell them, either in what he said with words, or by his actions. Somehow they were not always open to him. They heard and saw, but did not understand. We also can hear God speaking to us individually through the Bible which is his word, and through Jesus who is the Word made flesh; a word is always personal because it can only exist between persons. God also speaks to us through the liturgy, through sermons and in prayer, but like the disciples we do not always listen very attentively or understandingly. We have to learn to be open to God in such a way as to hear him when he speaks to us. Watching and praying go together!

By opening ourselves and our lives to God, we allow the Spirit whom he has given us to influence and help us understand the word he speaks through the channels just mentioned. He also speaks through the events of our lives, through people, through creation and in so many other things if we are alert and watching. But very often we do not believe that he speaks in these ways, so we do not hear. We just have a monologue with God, and not a conversation!

We have at some time or other to make an act of faith and accept that he does respond to us, and then remain open and attentive in prayer and watchful in life. We must believe Jesus, who lived so close to his Father that they were always in communication with each other, when he tells us that if we follow him he will lead us to the Father who will be, and is, in touch with us. And he gives us his Spirit so that we are helped to do this. All this is true, and we can experience the give and take of communicating with God in every aspect of our life if we let go of ourselves and respond. However God sometimes speaks by silence! This we can find very difficult to understand.

This leads to my third point, we get to know people by doing things with them. The disciples got to know Jesus through living their daily lives with him, and Jesus knew his Father by keeping in touch with him and living in accord with his will. The disciples were not very good at learning this way of living until Jesus was risen from the dead and the Holy Spirit had come to help them. We too, have to learn, how to live all our life in this sort of manner. I have tried to indicate how we can set about it in Chapter 3 in ways that, at first, at any rate, may seem contrived and rather mechanical, but which, if we persist, can eventually come to be second nature to us and can help us to live in the presence of God the whole time. We do all our work for God and as his will so as to please him. We may grow to have a background sense, or almost hidden sense, of being united, 'oned' to God in some manner. It can be like when we are in love with someone and we always have the loved person in mind without perhaps consciously adverting to them. This kind of continual awareness of God, which we may call praying without ceasing, is a disposition of heart that always inclines towards him. It seems to happen without our deliberately thinking about it; we become aware that the Holy Spirit prays in us and with us, and helps us continually in our living and praying.

Fourthly, we get to know people by learning about them with our minds. As I have frequently said, we have to read about how God has acted in the past with the Jews in the Old Testament, about what Jesus did and said in the New Testament, and what other of his followers have said throughout the ages as well as from those who wrote the Epistles and the *Acts of the Apostles*. We can also learn with our minds from the liturgies of the Church, as well as through observing the patterns of history. There are so many ways that God gives us to learn about him. Prayer needs to be fed, as it were, by such reading and meditating.

We must remember too that our minds do not work simply on their own, but they touch the whole of us, including our emotions. Learning with the mind includes pondering. 'Mary kept all these things, pondering on them in her heart'; the heart, the centre of our being, should be involved too. Knowing about someone involves ruminating on them, considering the mystery of their natures, getting the feel of them as we say. We must ruminate on God, Jesus, the Spirit, the Trinity by taking a bit of the Bible or the Creeds and chewing it over, as it were. Feeling, savouring, tasting and various other terms which are used to describe the responses of the senses, are applied to getting to know someone more deeply. We talk about getting the feel of a person, and we can do this by pondering on Jesus in a thoughtful manner. And when you have got the feel of a person, you can either respond to them or reject them; when you have read about Jesus Christ, you either go on to experience him more deeply or you look at him objectively and make no attempt to relate to him, and so reject the possibility of having a relationship with him.

Fifthly, I believe that you can get to know more about God through argument, through protesting about what happens, and through generally questioning him. We do this with our friends and the prophets did this. Jacob wrestled with the angel. It does not necessarily happen through words or through the kind of physical struggle Jacob had, though it may. You come before God and you tell him how unreasonable he seems to be being, or you can put your situation before him, and as it were, let him have you and it, and let him work on it. It is, perhaps, like wrestling of the more old fashioned sort; you sway to and fro ; or you lay a number of rather shapeless thoughts and ideas before God, and you and he hammer them into shape in the kind of way a blacksmith does with a bit of metal, making it into a horse-shoe or poker or whatever it is. Only it is us and our being that God is shaping. We give up something of our self-centredness, or as it were, surrender some part of ourselves, and God gives something of himself to us. It is a kind of give and take affair.

God takes and penetrates our being, but often in ways we do not see or understand at the time. As I have said Jacob was changed after his wrestling match, and had courage to face Esau whom he had feared to meet. Jacob knew he was limping after the encounter, but probably did not realise at the time how deeply the Lord had touched his inner being. When we argue with God with openness, we do not know how he is changing us and our view-points. Later we may get a glimmering of what has happened. We always want to see instant results. Through prayer that involves the whole of our being in honesty, we are more deeply touched by God than we imagine at the time.

The prophet Jeremiah is a good example of a person who argued and wrestled with the Lord. He was given the uncongenial task of telling his fellow-countrymen that they would be taken away captive into a foreign land because they had forsaken the Lord their God, who had sustained and kept them in the past. Jeremiah loved his people and did not wish this fate for them, nor did he want to deliver such a message because he was timid and sensitive and feared the repercussions on himself. He kept on telling God how hard it was, and how unhappy he was about it, yet he did what the Lord wanted. His conflicts and arguments with God helped to strengthen him and through them he learnt more about God, and how much the Lord loved him and his people. Deep down in his heart, he trusted his Lord, though he found him a difficult friend. God today too, very often seems to us to be a difficult and demanding friend.

When we are disputing with God, we must look at him as revealed in Jesus for he is the way which we must follow, though we may not understand how. The arguing or wrestling with God is bound to be wounding as our human wills are being taught and guided how to conform to the divine will. The deeper and more intimate the arguing, the deeper and more wounding will the pain be. But, as those who argue or wrestle know, even in defeat there is a certain exhilaration and pleasure.

Sometimes, however, God does not seem to want to wrestle. We go with things we want to ask and want to query, but he will not respond in any way. Then we have to lay the problem before him and get on with living, believing that 'he will be there as he will be there' though we may not know or perceive that he is there. For argumentative types this is very hard!

Seventhly, we can grow into being with God in prayer-times in companionable, loving silence in the way we do with a very close friend, or husband or wife. The ability to do this develops as we come to know a person well, and being together in companionable deep silence can be very wonderful and enriching. I have tried to show how this can happen with God in Chapters 7 and 8. The still and loving silence which we experience when we come close to God is even more wonderful, deep, and fulfilling than its human equivalent. We are silent because we feel so deeply that words would fail to convey what we feel.

Two people who get to know each other well can affect the thought and personality of the other, and sometimes besides having similar thoughts, they can somehow even come to look like each other. They are able to communicate without words, and sometimes do this over distances. God can communicate with us too in this silent almost imperceptible way.

Also if we live close to God, we can grow more like him and think and love in a similar kind of way to him. And we try to behave in the way we believe he wants us to, for our relationship with him makes even greater demands than any human one does as he expects more from us than any friend or lover. Jesus told those who wanted to follow him, 'If any man would come after me, let him deny himself and take up his cross and follow me . . . for whosoever loses his life for my sake and the gospel's will save it', (Mark 8.34-37).

What command could be more stringent than denying oneself? The change from becoming self-centred to become God-centred is demanding. But love for God will help us to do this, and the more we love God, the more we will want to please him and wish to be the kind of person he wants. Throughout all our life in relationship with God, we have to let him train and mould us in the way he wishes as well as disciplining ourselves to follow him. Probably in this book, I may not have seemed to stress very greatly the discipline that is required if we are to follow Christ and to live the kind of life he asks of us. I believe that it is through love for him and the power the Spirit gives us that we learn discipline and develop the wish to keep the commandments. However, when we first enter into a relationship with Christ, most of us have to make great efforts to keep the commandments and there seems to be very little love of the feeling kind connected with this. Frequently only a determination of the will seems to keep us at it. This, however, we must recognise as an important part of love. It is also much needed in marriage and it is what makes a marriage last through its dull and boring patches.

Also as you grow close to someone, you do not need

constant reassurance that they love you, though as we are human, a word of love now and then is pleasant and strengthening. However, you generally accept that you love each other and you live securely in this knowledge. This can happen with God if we are trusting enough; we realize that he never ceases to love and care for us however far away and distant he seems, and even when we have no sense of his presence. Sometimes this is not easy, especially if we have a feeling of emptiness in prayer time.

Certain attitudes are required if we are to get to know a person. We have to come to trust them. We have to realise that we are and will be in some way dependent on them and they on us, and that we will have to give something of ourselves to them. Loving is costly and often painful as well as joyous. Adapting to the other, giving up things which the other does not like or does not want us to do, makes demands on us. This upsets our self-centred and self-concerned selves but because of the friendship and love we have for the other, we are prepared to make sacrifices. Being dependent on the other also hurts our pride for we like to think that we are independent and can do everything for ourselves on our own. Pride is not realistic; the kind of humility which sees all men as interdependent and needing help from each other is simply accepting life as it is.

These attitudes are necessary when we relate to God in a deeper way. We have to trust God. It is difficult enough trusting someone we see, hear and touch, and can perceive how they react and think. We cannot see God face to face, and learning to trust someone whom we do not hear speak in ordinary human ways is not easy and demands great faith from us. We have to learn about his ways and what he wants from us through being attentive to him, particularly in prayer-time.

We also have to learn to be completely dependent on him. We are already whether we want to be or not, but we must realise that without him we can do nothing. Again it is not easy to believe this of someone you cannot see. It sounds difficult, well-nigh impossible. It would be if we were left on our own to do it, but we are not. We have Jesus Christ to show us the way to God the Father, and he not only shows us the way, but he is the way. This is not just a pleasing fancy or words that mean nothing, it is something which we can come to know by experience. Also he has given us his Spirit to pray with us and in us, and to show us how Jesus is the way. Without the gift of the Spirit to help us we would get nowhere. We must accept that we have been given this hidden power at our baptism, and if we avail ourselves of it, the Spirit will help and strengthen us if we give him the chance and take the risk of being guided and changed by him.

It is not easy, or really possible to explain how the Spirit works. He blows like a wind and in the direction he wishes, sometimes gently and sometimes with power. He changes people. The great Methodist preacher, Sangster, said that the Spirit turned the disciples from being frightened rabbits into ferrets. You may not like ferrets, who are cruel little animals, but they have courage and determination. The Holy Spirit gave the disciples courage and power to speak and preach about Jesus and his gospel, and completely changed them. He also made them speak in tongues, but this was just a fringe-benefit as it were, it was the change in their natures that mattered. They became Spirit-filled and God-centred. Jesus Christ gives us his Spirit to help us change into God-centred people if we will let him. It is in prayer time, when we are with God in openness, that the Spirit has more chance to awaken us to his presence. The Spirit can be the inspiration and main-spring of our prayer and life if we take the step that will give him freedom to act in us.

The difficult part is taking the first step. It seems to be a leap in the dark off the edge of something that may be a precipice; and God may not be holding a net below to catch us. Of course, it may not be a precipice. We do not know until we jump. We have in one way or another to let go of ourselves and let God take over.

This leap, for many is best taken in the daily prayer time where we must learn not to talk to God or think about him with our minds, but dare to stay for part of the time quiet, and attentive to him. We have to remain there in trust, letting the Spirit of God work in us, and believe that he will. We will have to let him lead wherever he wishes, however strange the way may seem. We must not fear, but believe and know that he is with us, strengthening us and he will not give us more to bear than we are able.

The Spirit really does help us to follow Jesus, and gives us power so that we can be God-centred rather than self-centred. He, William of Saint Thierry says is the love the Father and Son love each other with, and through living in us, he draws us into this eternal Trinity of love so that we can experience the action of the Trinity in our prayer. This may sound fanciful, but if we let him, he gives us the ability to love God in a way that we never believed was possible. Each of us has to take the plunge and say 'yes' to this love. Some say 'yes' without almost realising when and how, but many have to consciously hand-over to God. The sort of love the Spirit gives makes us forget the cost in human terms and the pains that being shaped by Love into the sort of person that God wants us to be, may bring. This love leads to that deep kind of peace which would seem to be in the heart of the unity of the Godhead; it is the peace that passes all understanding. This kind of love can never be idle but requires us to go out in love to our neighbour. Prayer that is centred on God, prayer where the Spirit is the main-spring of our action, must have fruition in a love of our fellow creatures that is active and creative.

The ruling motive of Christ's life was his Father's will and his service of mankind stemmed from this. 'I am coming down from heaven not to do my will, but the will of him that sent me' (Jn. 6.38). Somehow the will of God seems to be more than God's purpose for mankind and creation; it would appear to be the driving force of his very being. It is life-giving and it asks from us dynamic action rather than passive acceptance.

Jesus Christ wishes us to have unity of will with the Father and to be one with him. In this close father and child relationship which touches us most deeply in prayer, we catch something of the dynamism of the will of God which sends us out to serve him in the world and in our relationships with others. In his will is our peace, our joy, our very life!

Appendix
Stages in Prayer

Wordless, imageless prayer, quiet prayer, contemplation or whatever one likes to call it, as I have already said, had, until recently been regarded as the prerogative of a kind of spiritual élite. You had to leave the world to become a hermit or enter an enclosed religious order to qualify. But now people living ordinary lives in the world seem to pray this way, or at any rate in a much less wordy way than had been usual previously. I have suggested that probably a number of people of a loving and simple nature have prayed in this manner throughout the ages, but as they were not literate, few educated persons realised their existence. People of more education in the Catholic tradition were deterred from this kind of prayer by books and priests who decreed that it was not for them. Some Protestant groups had either never heard of this kind of prayer or regarded it as a kind of self-deception. For example, Mary Slessor, a saintly Scottish Presbyterian missionary in Africa, found her spontaneous prayer had gone dead, and when she sought advice was told just to keep at it, whereas it could have been, one imagines, an indication that she should have been guided in to a more wordless kind of prayer. Her friends either did not know of contemplation or, if they did, disapproved of it.

The reasons why the authorities frowned on this sort of prayer are somewhat tangled and complicated. One reason certainly was that a scheme of spiritual growth had been formulated, and it was thought that it had to be followed stage by stage, and in a certain order. The notion of purgative, illuminative and unitive stages as indicating a successive development in the spiritual life was generally accepted in the middle ages, and the unitive stage was linked with contemplative prayer and regarded as suitable only for a chosen few.

Also as I have tried to indicate, there grew up in the middle ages a spirituality which was centred on the man Jesus. Those who followed this way often did not appear to recognise that Jesus who is both man and God, is the way to the Father. Seeing Jesus in isolation and not as the way to the Father can lead to spiritual stagnation; all relationship with God has to be on-going but it withers if one stays static or goes backwards. A number of people seem also to have forgotten about the Holy Spirit who helps us in our journey to the Father. God-centred, wordless and imageless prayer came to be regarded by some of these people as wrong because they could not see the place of Jesus in it though the great Franciscan theologian Saint Bonaventure had shown that the cross was the taking off point for the leap into the darkness of God and contemplative prayer. The history of the struggle which developed between the two kinds of Christians became complicated at the end of the seventeenth century when Quietism which was associated with God-centred wordless prayer, was condemned. Meditation on the mysteries of the faith became the rule, and this was regarded as a defence against illuminism and individualism by the Catholic church. Also at that time the growing spirit of rationalism in Europe was anti-mystical and helped to discredit a spirituality which appeared to give reason a secondary place. People who prayed wordlessly and imagelessly in a God-centred way had, as it were, to go underground, and this kind of prayer only began to be considered respectable at the end of the nineteenth century possibly as a result of more interest being taken in Greek patristic writers including Pseudo-Dionysius, and with him Neo-Platonism. Auguste Sandreau, Augustin Poulain and Henri Bremond in France and Dean Inge[1] in England helped to revive interest in mystical spirituality. Baron von Hügel, Abbot Chapman and Evelyn Underhill have been responsible for interpreting the work of the spiritual experts of the past for a wider public in England. However there has always remained in France, Italy and Germany a few writers in the contemplative tradition though their work was necessarily guarded. Among them were de Caussade and Grou whose writings are being found helpful again today. Amongst the Puritans the tradition was maintained at least in the seventeenth and early eighteenth centuries and has continued among the Quakers, though it has been foreign to many of the Protestant bodies. It has reappeared from time to time in the Anglican tradition particularly in periods when the early fathers were being studied. People who accepted the possibility of contemplative prayer have, until very recently, linked it

1. Dean Inge in the preface of the seventh edition of *Christian Mysticism* writes, 'The other cause which led to careful study of mysticism is the new science of Psychology'.

with the stages in the spiritual ascent evolved in the middle ages.

The notion of purgative, illuminative and unitive stages[2] seems to have come from the idea current in the patristic period that the Christian had need for reform in the moral sphere, for development of knowledge of God or illumination in the intellectual and emotional spheres, and prayer, all of which combined to unify man in himself and unite him with God. The whole personality was embraced in a movement that led towards knowing and loving God more closely and becoming more like him. The division of this threefold unity into three separate stages tended to break up something which should be regarded as a whole. Bonaventure, Ruysbroeck and some of the other great medieval spiritual writers saw this danger and tried to indicate how the three parts or stages were concurrent rather than successive, but in attempting to do this their writings became so complicated as to be almost incomprehensible to non-medieval man who is not trained in their way of thought. It is certainly not easy to try to show how the three sides of Christian growth fit in with each other, but I believe it is important to do so.

In the Christian life, moral reform and the disciplining of the will are necessary throughout life; Saint Paul tells us that we need to go into training for the Christian life in the kind of way athletes train for their sports and soldiers for their job. Disciplined preparation is essential to bring us back to our aim in life which should be

2. People in the first stage, or way, of life were sometimes called beginners, those in the second proficients (people who were progressing), and those in the third, perfect.

loving union with God. So we have to try to root out our vices and to develop virtues. Many people start by doing this, and, at the beginning of their life as followers of Christ, take much time and give great attention to it, but it is a process that has to go on as long as we live, though the more united we are to God, the less conscious we are of doing it. We also learn that without God's help we can achieve little, and it is by increasing love of him that an interior impetus is given to outward reforms. Illumination helps us to love in this kind of way. So at all stages we have to use our minds to read, or learn and think about God and Jesus who is the way to him, and so illumine our minds to make us want to love him more. We have to know the God we are learning to love. In prayer, we should grow in love for God, and gradually our union with him should become closer for the stage, which came to be known as unitive, is the fullest development of what was called 'prayer' by the Fathers. These three elements of the Christian life, purification, illumination, and union interpenetrate, and progress has to be made in all of them concurrently. However, at certain periods of growth each of these will have a different emphasis, and one may seem to predominate over the others. The first two are bound to influence prayer which is the third. What we are outside of prayer will affect how we pray, and how we pray and relate to God should affect the way we live.

It is no use thinking that we can reform ourselves by our own efforts. It often seems to me that some spiritual writers have made it appear as if we could. The Jews appear to have made the keeping of the law something they did themselves and Jesus condemned the Pharisees for setting about it in this way. It is only by being in touch with God (in prayer time and in life, for our relationship with God should never be broken) and by letting the Spirit help us that we can be reformed in a way that affects our inner being. The purification comes from our cooperation with the Spirit who initiates the process in us. We are 'fellow workers' with Christ in this. What we are affects how we live. Love for God and love for man should touch all our living and lead to the reform of our conduct. By co-operating with the Spirit our very natures are purified, and this alone can change our way of life. So getting to know God in prayer, responding to him, becoming more united to him, and letting his light touch our hearts and minds is the best way to reform our conduct. The Spirit has to act in us and with us so as to help us grow more like Jesus.

We are all different and God calls us or draws us to him in varying ways. Some people, he touches with love at the start of their serious Christian lives and they have, in prayer, at the very beginning a close sense of union with him. They, as it were, commence near the end of the so-called Christian ascent or progress. If this is so, they will have to undertake the other two sides of the Christian life, they will have to be reformed or purified and they will have to learn about the God, who has drawn them to him. The illuminative aspect has to touch the mind and the heart in some way or other too, for knowledge and love of God are both necessary. Other people appear to have to plug away at reforming their lives seemingly without much inspiration or illumination by God, and if this is so, they will have to meditate or read about him, and pray, and keep on until he illumines them in one way or another.

Progress in prayer has, usually in the West, been measured by the way a person prayed; vocal prayer was regarded as a lower form than mental, and wordless, conceptless prayer as the highest, and one has to progress from the one form to the other in that order. However as we do not pray to become better prayers, but in order to know and love God more deeply and in order to learn to respond to him, I believe the content and intention of the prayer is more important than the form. The main thing is to want to change from being self-centred to being God-centred. The form we pray in will probably depend on our personality, our environment and the age we live in, and above all the way the Spirit leads. What was the norm for the seventeenth century will not necessarily be best for today.

Western Christianity can benefit from the teaching of the early Eastern fathers and from Eastern Orthodoxy. Stages of prayer for the Desert fathers sometimes seems to have been based on 1 Timothy 2.1 where we are exhorted to practice petitions, prayers, intercessions and thanksgivings. These represent the attitude and thought of the person praying vis a vis God. Alongside this, as I have shown earlier in this chapter, and parallel with it, went moral purification, and the purification of the senses, the imagination and the intelligence.

Petitions or supplications, the first stage, were mainly connected with confession of sins and prayers for pardon. The Christian was awed by the fear of the Lord and with this went a re-ordering of life in conformity with his commandments. This is the equivalent of the purgatorial stage and restores man to a right relationship with God. The second, 'prayers', seems to cover a period when the soul was asking God for virtues and graces, and is the beginning of self-dedication. This corresponds in part to the positive side of the so-called purgatorial stage but would also seem to overlap with the illuminative. With intercessions, the third stage, the Christian becomes more concerned with God and his own relationship with others and develops compassion to his neighbour, i.e. God is acting through him. This should be a feature of the illuminative life. The fourth stage is thanksgiving and adoration. The soul is so overwhelmed with love of God and his goodness that these themes form a dominant note in life and prayer, and concern for self is virtually forgotten. This is characteristic of the unitive life. Of course all the themes which make up the four stages ought to occur in all prayer but with changing emphasis.

The Eastern tradition perhaps has laid less stress on the form of prayer and allowed greater flexibility according to the individual and his circumstances. It is, however, pointed out that oral prayer must involve the mind, for one would not be praying unless one understood the words one was using. The best prayer is that in which 'the mind is brought into the heart'. As I have suggested (Chap. 2) the heart is the centre of unity in man where he meets God and where the Spirit acts in him. There are two kinds of prayer of the heart, the *strenuous* where man himself strives for it (acquired contemplation) and the *self-impelled* when the prayer acts on its own (infused); the prayer offers itself spontaneously and is given to man as a gift. This kind of prayer goes beyond consciousness. In the prayer of the heart, the mind, affection and the whole personality seems to be taken up with God, as it is in the highest kind of contemplation in the western tradition, though there appears to be feeling in it. This kind of feeling though it is refined and transformed by grace remains feeling. Joy, light, tenderness, warmth and so on can colour or come into the prayer, and this is accepted as being right in the Eastern tradition, though it has often been frowned upon in the West. Of course it must not be sought for as an experience nor possessed[3]. I believe it can be a feature in Western contemplation too but as feelings have tended to be discredited, people have often refrained from admitting to them!

The notion of stages, it will be noted, seems also to feature in the Eastern Christian approach, even if they are not so much tied to specific forms such as vocal, mental and contemplative prayer. The progress, however, is connected with the degree of self-giving in the prayer.

The Christian has to grow in openness to God, to his neighbour, and to creation as a whole. This is essential for Christians of all traditions though how they begin may vary. Some may start with the neighbour, some with God, and others with self-reform. Today younger people are more concerned with their neighbours and the under-privileged of the world than they are with self-reform and their own salvation. People in the past have often been so taken up with saving their own souls that they have not been concerned with God or their neighbour.

3. See *The Art of Prayer* compiled by Igumen Chariton of Valamo and edited with an introduction by Timothy (Kallistos) Ware, London, 1966.

They have been occupied with fighting temptations rather than seeking God and have been concerned with a 'glory-for-me' rather than a 'glory-for-God' religion! God's glory and God's work must be our concern, and not ourselves. They also saw moral reform as something they did, and did not recognise that only God can give us the power to overcome our failings and sins.

Perhaps it is because young people today are more given to helping their neighbours than to adoring, serving, and praising God that their prayer is often simple and wordless and akin to contemplation. They, as it were, start from a different point on the spiritual course. All parts of the course will have to be covered, rather like runners who start from different places in a race but ultimately cover the same ground. We all have to be purified, illumined and united to God, but how and when may vary considerably.

To return to the traditional Western scheme of spiritual progress, since the sixteenth century, it has been stressed that the third stage, the Unitive (where contemplative prayer was regarded as the norm), is reached by a more radical dying to self than any that has gone before. This dying is initiated by God though man must be ready to respond to God's action as fully as he is able. At this point in the scheme, normal human ways of acting (i.e. thinking, imagining, loving etc.) cease to be possible. Needless to say this change is, in various degrees, painful and bewildering. This dying has been known since the time of Saint John of the Cross as the dark night of the senses and is seen as being both active and passive.[4] Saint Bonaventure put it rather differently and, perhaps, for some more clearly in the *Itinerarium mentis in Deum* where he showed that man had to die with Christ on the cross in order to go with him to the Father. It was a terrific, purging *transitus,* a going over, a passing over, and was painful at the time but, in the end, joyous. 'He who loves this death can see God, for it is absolutely true that none shall see me and live' (Chap. 7). The experience is darkness to man because of the transcendence of God and because of the impossibility of knowing him by the normal human, created faculties. The way of knowledge and union with God was through Christ (both God and man), by going with him through death to resurrection and union with the Father. Dionysius the Pseudo-Areopagite had also emphasised the necessity of purification before God could be known in the dazzling darkness of conceptless prayer. Most authors have stressed that the passage to the unitive stage is distressing. Growth is always painful but many who are in the Eastern Orthodox spiritual tradition do not emphasise the pain because they are overwhelmed by the joy of the union which is full of warmth and

4. According to Saint John of the Cross there are two main nights, one of the senses and another of the spirit. Dr. Truman Dicken in his book *The Crucible of Love* indicates that for Saint John 'dark night' does not refer to a passing phase, still less to a transitory experience of the spiritual life, for there is only one night as this is the saint's term for privation, eradication of all that is not God. It is by this progressively complete privation that the soul is emptied of all that can fill it to the exclusion of God. However the night is usually divided into stages. The first, known as that of the senses, comes when a person can no longer pray using the intellect and imagination, and the second, the night of the spirit, when all delight in spiritual things is lost, and God seems far off and separated from the soul.

light. As I have said feelings of this nature have not been downgraded as they have so often in the west.[5] In the West certain writers of the Flemish and German schools stressed the pain in such a way as almost to exclude any thought of joy, possibly because they believed that the material world was evil whereas the Orthodox see it as God's creation which is being redeemed along with mankind.

In the West the change to the unitive stage was usually indicated when prayer that used words, concepts or images became impossible. People could not meditate but found themselves seemingly empty of thought, but yet longing for God in an obscure manner. The change from the ways that they had been used to was very disturbing, and at a later stage they frequently thought themselves deserted by God who seemed not only sometimes to be absent, but also to be threatening. All this, often as well as privations, bad health, ill fortune, and so on had to be endured in faith. This faith was lacking in emotion or intellectual content; it was a naked stretching to God, a kind of clinging to a hidden God.

For some today, as I have already suggested the situation is different and the usual pattern of progress does not seem to be followed. They are given simple wordless prayer quite near the beginning of their serious prayer life, and though it may be bewildering, it is often comforting and strengthening. The transition to simple prayer for them is somewhat different. For some of these people a complete change still occurs and they

5. Kallistos Ware in *The Power of the Name*, however, indicates how certain of the desert Fathers regarded certain stages of prayer as 'a hidden martyrdom'.

are simplified by God and led to operate on a plane above the ordinary human one so that they may learn to encounter God in union unfettered by self-preoccupation. It is still a way of bare faith, that is faith which is unassisted by reason or emotion, and it can be bewildering and purifying. Some people who are led into this way by God have undergone much pain and distress before they even came to believe in God at all. God for them had been Walt Whitman's 'You whoever you are' and it was only when they were given deep prayer by God that they came to believe in him at all in an accepted way. The pain of unbelief that they had experienced before may have been a kind of dark night. Others may have suffered from a sense of alienation or from a lack of sense of identity. These kind of people will have to be brought to know the Christ of the gospels, and the Christ who gives himself in the sacraments, and they will have in some way or other to undergo moral purification. As I have already said the whole spiritual course has to be covered sometime and this will have to be made plain to such people. Spiritual progress in a non-Christian world can appear to be topsy-turvy to devotees of the traditional scheme of spiritual progress, but the Spirit fortunately has never been tied to schemes. Also I think there is a tendency for us to experience what we expect to experience. The tradition in which we were nurtured influences the way we grow, and there is nothing wrong in this. The Spirit, however, often disrupts our traditional pattern, and many who pray today, have no tradition at all

The way the change to unitive prayer occurs varies with each individual. Usually the more conventional practising Christian sees that his old ways of trying to love God were inadequate without realising that there are others that are deeper and closer. Quite often this realisation is twofold. It is objective; this is manifested in the distance or absence of God. It is also subjective; the soul sees its own weakness and imperfection. Today the objective aspect is often connected with unbelief. God has not simply withdrawn to test our love; it is no longer a game of love as it appeared to be to medieval writers. God seems not to exist. It is quite impossible for such people to believe intellectually that there is a God. The fear that all one's previous experience of God in prayer has been delusion and that there is no God, only a void, is terrifying. Concern now is not for one's personal salvation, but rather for the whole of creation which is seen as unordered and pointless. Nevertheless before close union with God some such experience, often prolonged, is usual. The subjective side which is manifested by the weakness, hopelessness, and helplessness of the self remains a feature of this stage and is as seemingly unbearable as in previous ages. Bare faith is still the one thing needed, and this should be combined with the surrender of oneself and acceptance of the circumstances or changes which God brings. Sometimes, too, liturgical or communal worship, which is generally such a support to the individual worshipper when in distress, seems useless and empty. The sense of belonging to the people of God is completely removed.

In this period of transition a spiritual guide or director is invaluable. But often one of the trials is the inability to find anyone who understands one's predicament.

I have discussed the distresses that befall people who are being led by the Spirit to closer union with God in some detail because they often get glossed over today. People are afraid of pain and discipline. Pain is part of the dying with Christ so as to be able to live again with him. The Christian pattern is always one of death and resurrection. The joy that we have after the distress makes us forget the pain in a way similar to the pains of childbirth which are soon forgotten once they are over. Living the resurrection life with Christ is joyous though sometimes the joy is intertwined with pain.

I want to return to the people who do not follow the traditional pattern of spiritual growth. Some today who have not been brought up as Christians in a traditional way, as I have suggested, get led to silent, wordless prayer without having practised vocal prayer or meditation which in the past was regarded as the correct way to such contemplation. Either a silence, obviously God-given, falls on their conversation with God or Jesus, or they are led quietly to an almost silent adoration which may be punctuated by short ejaculations. The greater part of the purgatorial stage seems to be missed. Purification will ultimately come in other ways, I think we may be sure of this, though whether it will be as bitter and painful as some Western Christians in the past have suggested, one cannot say.

As I have suggested some of these people who seem to start with simple prayer centred on God, may not have learnt to know and love Christ of the gospels in the way previous generations did through meditation and Bible reading. Somehow they will have to be taught to know the Jesus of the gospels and to associate him with the God they experience in prayer. Set meditation of the old type may not be of use to them, but prayerful pondering on the gospel may be of more help. The kind of sermons or homilies that are preached by people who have a real, living relationship with Jesus, can be most instructive and helpful for them. As in the case of the development of human relationships, the experience of getting to know Christ must involve the mind to some degree (that is be in some way intellectual), but also must be a genuine personal contact, an experience, that touches the whole man. If the person belongs to a Christian community that is sacramentally based, the Eucharist will be of great importance as affording unique opportunities for encountering Christ personally. Dionysius, the Pseudo-Areopagite, stressed that the same Christ was the content, as well as the inspirer, of the Scriptures, of apostolic preaching and of the sacraments, and particularly of the Eucharist. The meeting at the Eucharist of the risen and glorified Christ, both immanent and transcendent, can lead to a greater personal experience of him who gives himself freely to us here. In the Eastern Orthodox liturgies the balance between the crucified and risen Christ, God imminent and God transcendent, and God in Trinity, is more clearly expressed than it is in Western liturgies though it is also recognisable here. The important aspect of the liturgy, for those who have come to wordless and imageless prayer not by the way of the Son, is that there is a unique opportunity for a person to person contact with him here. So sacramental and personal prayer can come to fuse into each other. Prayer, meditation on the Scriptures, and worship can and should interpenetrate each other and form a unity, and this is true for every Christian. Perhaps if they are led to know Christ in these ways they will come to realise that they are supported and helped by the Spirit.

Today there are people who start with the Spirit, and some may want to stay with the Spirit, though generally he seems to lead them to praise the Father and/or the Son. However, their preference can be for the Spirit and particularly for his gifts, but the giver is greater than his gifts. The greatest gift that he can give is love; love that will unite us with the Father and the Son. Again, however, knowledge must go with love and people who are devoted to the Spirit will have to learn more about the Son.

This starting with God or the Spirit, rather than following Jesus as the way to the Father with the Spirit helping, can affect a person's attitude to the Trinity. Also those who see Jesus in isolation and not as the way to the Father, will, of course, not know God the Father, nor will those who cling to the Spirit alone. Belief in the Trinity grew out of Christian experience of the Three Persons and their unity, and early credal formulas were attempts to express this in thought forms that were intelligible to people of their times. And again today the Trinity and Unity can, and should, be known by experience, though it is not easy to express this in words or explain how it comes about. Below I try to show how people have known and experienced the Trinity and Unity in unitive prayer (p. 186f).

It may be useful now to look at the various descriptions of unitive prayer which we can arrive at by all the ways which I have touched on. Generally when this prayer is reached we cease to be aware that we are praying but realise that God is praying in us or as Orthodox writers have said 'We become prayer'[1]. It is no longer self-conscious, and we can no longer say 'Look at me I'm praying'.

In Julian Slade's musical *Salad Days,* people when they come to the magic piano and find they can play it, sing 'Look at me I'm playing'. When God takes over our prayer, infuses it, we can be tempted to say to ourselves 'Look at me I'm praying'; the break through comes when we forget to do this!

When one comes to live more closely to God in what may be called the unitive way there is much more variety in the prayer than is generally indicated. People who have been able to describe their experience of the prayer of union have usually been highly individual, often forceful characters. Saint Teresa of Avila's union has frequently been accepted as the norm, and the account of her spiritual marriage taken as the highest union possible. One would almost think her relationship with God hardly changed after this. Her perception of the Trinity which appears to come later in her life has sometimes caused difficulty to those who have tried to evolve a scheme from her writings, though this perception is often the outcome of unitive prayer. In fact anything may happen once the break-through into the unitive

1. cf. Paul Evdokimov 'In the catacombs the image that recurs most frequently is the figure of a woman in prayer, the *orans.* It represents the only true attitude of the human soul. It is not enough to *possess* prayer; we must *become* prayer, prayer incarnate', quoted by Kallistos Ware in *The Power of the Name,* Fairacres, Oxford, 1974.

stage has been made. Nevertheless any Christian may have brief experience of the unitive way of life at any period of his spiritual growth. These experiences are often in flashes. When they occur early on they can help stimulate love of God and inspire one to undertake the purifications which are usually necessary before union becomes more or less consciously continuous.

The experience of union known in the latter stages of spiritual growth is very difficult to describe as it occurs on a plane above normal ways of acting or in a part of the human personality not usually consciously recognised[6]. It is, therefore, impossible to give a clear-cut account of unitive prayer, firstly because of the difficulty of finding words even remotely adequate to express it, and secondly because each person who tries, has to do it in a way suitable to his own intellect, character, age, etc. and in terms of the times in which he is living. Also prayer may vary considerably from day to day though one's union with God remains stable throughout daily activity. Also in close union one's self-consciousness can leave one for comparatively long periods. This experience becomes so much part of one that any attempt to describe it is difficult because to do so it is necessary to become self-conscious again, and so the resulting description is only partial. As I have said God takes over and the prayer just happens – we become the prayer.

However several ways of indicating close union with God have kept recurring throughout the Christian era. The Eastern Fathers called the experience

6. These two forms of expression are used by spiritual writers to imply the ineffable nature of the experience, and seems to mean the same thing.

deification. Athanasius taught that Christ by becoming man has made it possible for us, through him, to become God. We put on Christ, or Christ is born in us in such a way that we no longer live but Christ lives in us. The Eastern Fathers expressed this in a number of different ways. William of Saint Thierry, who was much influenced by these fathers, also saw close union as deification and sometimes explained it in terms of union of wills. Through unity of our will with God's will we come to will only what God wills. This form of expression for union has occurred less frequently in the West, though Benet of Canfield, a sixteenth century Capucin, used it very effectively. Now that there is closer contact with the Orthodox church, spiritual writers seem less afraid to describe union in terms of deification, which it must be noted does not mean that we lose our individuality but rather our personality becomes permeated by God as iron becomes red hot in fire.

Another description of unitive prayer already mentioned is dazzling darkness. We realise that we are experiencing what might be called a vision of God, but because of our human condition and the greatness and infinity of God we cannot define the vision. The brightness of his glory blurs our sight but we somehow know that it is wonderful and all that could possibly be desired, though it is also unknowing and darkness. Despite the fact that the experience affects the whole personality and all aspects of life, it can rarely be clearly recalled. It is something that we can never get enough of and something that we constantly long for. The great patristic writers called this half-satisfied and ever-increasing desire *epectasis*. This term indicates how it is impossible to stand still in the spiritual life, we always have to reach forward to try to apprehend God (cf. Philippians 3.14), for our experience of God makes us long to know him more. There is no union so close that it cannot be closer, and God, if we allow him, increases our capacity to receive him. *Epectasis* is connected with the eschatological element in Christianity, i.e. the Kingdom has come and is with us, but we are still expecting it in its fullness for we are, at the moment, only pilgrims on earth.

A third way of describing the unitive stage is by using terms connected with marriage which are frequently based on the *Song of Songs*. People of an affectionate temperament often employ this form of description. Though Origen used the *Song of Songs* to illustrate union with God, the description of the soul's union with God as marriage was first fully developed in the West in the middle ages as a result of the writing and preaching of Saint Bernard, and the writings of Hugh of Saint Victor and William of Saint Thierry. The spouse of the *Song of Songs* is often associated with Jesus, sometimes with him as the Lamb. This kind of union tends to be Christo-centric.[7] Again there is in some writers, especially those following Gregory of Nyssa and Origen, the idea of the Bridegroom coming to the soul in darkness and then leaving it so that the soul is frequently

7. F. Vernet in *Medieval Spirituality*, London, 1930, commenting on the nuptial imagery, writes; 'Certain expressions made use of by the mystics concerning the marriage between God and the soul seem to us today somewhat hazardous and disconcerting . . . to medieval writers that ancient love poem, the Canticle of Canticles, had become through its commentaries as virginal as the Alpine heights'!

in a state of longing for the Bridegroom.[8]

A fourth way of describing the prayer of union is in association with the Trinity. Sometimes this is seen as a kind of participation in the life of the Trinity, and at other times as an intellectual enlightenment about the nature of the Trinity, though the latter may follow on after the kind of experience just mentioned. William of Saint Thierry, himself here following Saint Augustine, has greatly influenced the form of expression relating to the experience of union that is closely associated with the Trinity. William believed that because of the Incarnation of the Son, the Holy Spirit working in us is able to restore to us the Trinitarian image of God and enable us through him — the love with which the Father and Son love each other — to participate in some manner in the life of the Trinity without damaging its transcendence. Such a knowledge of God within us is not a self-regarding introversion, but a way of worshipping and loving God in a manner similar to that in which the Persons of the Trinity love each other, and which excludes any self-consciousness. Another expression of Trinitarian union visualises the soul as resting in the Godhead in love (fruition) as well as going out in active deeds of charity to others in a way that parallels the activity of the Persons of the Trinity. The rest in God where the soul is closely united with God is the source of charity and apostolicity. The Holy Spirit is again regarded as being our inspiration and the link which enables us to share in some way in the life of the Godhead. Ruysbroeck is the clearest and most inspiring exponent of this type of union. The way

8. Gregory of Nyssa writes: 'I have had the love of my beloved but he escapes my thoughts.'

to it is through Christ but the actual rest in God is described in terms of unknowing — it is neither 'this nor that' and the 'unknowing is inaccessible light'. The Trinitarian explanations of union combine Christo-centric and Theo-centric approaches through the Spirit in a balanced way, and also love and intellect fuse in a kind of union which involves the whole personality.

Fifthly and often connected either with the Trinitarian approach or with the way of unknowing is the description of union as loss in God; we forget ourselves in God, all of our being and life get dropped into the enfolding abyss of the Godhead, yet the personality is not lost but somehow grows to be more truly itself. Most people who describe union in the ways just mentioned, stress the point that in union a man does not lose his individuality but rather that it is developed and reformed in the pattern which God wishes for it.

There are, of course, many other ways of describing unitive prayer.

Several conclusions about this prayer may be drawn. Firstly though it is very hard to put into words, it can be one of the most real and abiding things in a person's life. The perception of union, whatever form it takes, may leave one seemingly in darkness, but God in some way or other sends his Spirit to help one persist. For example Saint Jeanne de Chantal for most of her latter years was in complete darkness and desolation, yet she persisted in prayer and in some indefinable way knew that this was right. She knew and experienced her own emptiness and helplessness. Secondly the experience of unitive prayer drives one on to seek for closer union with

God however crucifying the way may be. Union in fact
would seem to be only possible through Christ crucified.
Darkness and pains similar to those known in the dark
nights preceding union can keep recurring. Thirdly
prayer does not stay the same but varies with our
physical condition, external circumstances and with
God's plan for bringing us into closer union with him.
There is rarely any sense of progress and often one can
seem to be regressing. Progress in this kind of prayer is
like climbing a high and complex, mountain, and one
has frequently to descend into a valley before another
ascent can be made. Fourthly, we and our prayer
become simplified, and with this goes a wonderful sense
of freedom. Prayer is usually wordless and silent; it is an
experience of God which makes us know we are one with
him and leads to adoration. However we have to use the
means of communication with him which he gives us and
this may be silence, or involve words, sighs, loving glances,
or 'a naked intent' stretching to him. Usually we have
little choice and have to 'pray as we can' and not to
pray as we can't.[9] One of the things unitive prayer
teaches is how to respond to the movement of the
Spirit which may lead us anywhere. Fifthly prayer and
life become one and the same; all life is prayer, and
prayer contains all of our life, drawing into it every
aspect of our personality and daily life.

It is probably that the great diversity of the prayer
of union has not always been recognised in the west
where often silent contemplation has been taken to be
the norm for the third stage. This prayer, however,

9. cf. *The Spiritual Letters* of John Chapman, ed. R. Huddlestone,
O.S.B, London, 1954, p.109.

dissociated as it is from the usual ways of operation of
the faculties, is in some way different from any other.
In the unitive way, because of radical deaths of the self,
God is able to act in and through the soul in ways not
possible before. Those, who have not allowed God to
work these deaths in them, may think that they have
reached the unitive way, and for this reason, western
spiritual writers have urged caution about those who
should be allowed to read books written specifically for
it. Eastern Orthodox writers have done this less, probably
because they less frequently depict spiritual growth in
clear-cut stages and tend to stress concurrently the need
for moral purification, intellectual growth in knowledge
of God, together with a deepening relationship in
prayer. All these must be employed together to make
close union possible.

To conclude, unitive prayer is the most complete
self-giving which is possible to the soul and is the most
complete giving of God that the soul is able to receive at
the time of giving. So we end with the fourth and
highest theme of the Eastern tradition, thanksgiving and
adoration. But as Richard of Saint Victor, Ruysbroeck
and many others have said, the deeper the experience of
God, the more a person is compelled to go out in love to
help his neighbour, and the highest stage is when a person
is so closely and habitually united to God that the love
God gives him cannot be idle but impels him to love and
care for others.